STUDY GUIDE

BY MARY-ELAINE SWANSON

TO

THE CHRISTIAN HISTORY OF THE CONSTITUTION OF THE UNITED STATES OF AMERICA

VOLUME II
CHRISTIAN SELF-GOVERNMENT WITH UNION

COMPILED BY VERNA M. HALL

PUBLISHED BY

AMERICAN CHRISTIAN HISTORY INSTITUTE
PALO CEDRO, CALIFORNIA

ANNO DOMINI 1988

To obtain additional copies of this Study Guide,
write to the publishers:

AMERICAN CHRISTIAN HISTORY INSTITUTE
P.O. Box 648
Palo Cedro, California 96073

Printed in the United States of America

International Standard Book Number:
0-9616201-0-2

DEDICATION

VERNA M. HALL
American Christian Historian

May we fulfill

the purpose of her great lifework

and accept our responsibility to restore

America's Christian History and government

to our homes, schools and churches.

"... and let her own works praise her in the gates."

Proverbs 31:31

ACKNOWLEDGMENTS

My deep gratitude and appreciation go to Mr. and Mrs. John G. Talcott, Jr., without whose vision and financial support this *Study Guide* would not have been possible.

To Miss Rosalie J. Slater, President of the Foundation for American Christian Education, my warmest appreciation for her gracious permission to adapt the "seven-step" method she used for the *Christian History Study Course* in her trail-blazing book, *Teaching and Learning America's Christian History: The Principle Approach.* In the Principle Approach, Miss Slater has rediscovered and redefined the historic method of education employed by our forefathers and has set valuable precedents for American Christian education today.

To my colleague, Mr. James B. Rose, President of the American Christian History Institute, I owe a special debt of gratitude for his insights as a Master Teacher of the Principle Approach and his invaluable support and suggestions during the writing of this *Study Guide.*

My thanks are also extended to Miss Katherine Dang, Treasurer of F.A.C.E., and Administrator of Chinese Christian Schools, San Leandro, California, for taking the time in her busy life to read the manuscript of the *Guide* and offer helpful suggestions from her experience as a historian and Principle Approach teacher.

Particular mention should also be made of Mrs. Desta Garrett, F.A.C.E.'s typographer *par excellence,* whose careful and conscientious attention to detail are much appreciated.

Mary-Elaine Swanson

FOREWORD

America's Christian history documents that when the Bible became available to the individual, a voluntary spiritual unity (or oneness of the separate parts), consisting of a common faith and knowledge of Christ's love and law, eventually produced both the spirit and fact of American political union.

When the unity of Christian faith and practice reached America with the Pilgrims in 1620, their spirit of voluntary association became the foundation of voluntary political union by covenant or compact. This voluntary political union was inspired by "the Pilgrim ideal of a 'single covenanted body of Christians, united for *civil* as well as *spiritual* purposes.'" (*Teaching and Learning America's Christian History, The Principle Approach (T & L),* by Rosalie J. Slater, p. 268)

Now, the Christian principle of American political union, as documented in Volume II of *The Christian History of the Constitution: Christian Self-Government with Union,* by Verna M. Hall, has been elucidated through the Christian scholarship and diligence of Mary-Elaine Swanson, a researcher and writer well qualified for the task. Perhaps best known as the co-author with Marshall Foster of the book and film, *The American Covenant — The Untold Story,* Mrs. Swanson has been a student of America's Christian history and government for nearly thirty years. She worked closely with Miss Hall when the original resources used in Volume I of *The Christian History of the Constitution: Christian Self-Government* were being compiled and wrote the concise biographical sketches of the historians whose work was used in that first volume. She also contributed more biographies to Miss Hall's historic compilation, *The Christian History of the American Revolution: Consider and Ponder.* Equipped with a background in journalistic writing and research and a unique English heritage, she has lectured and written on the history of liberty and civil government for the Mayflower Institute and now for the American Christian History Institute.

The reader will discover in this *Study Guide* Mrs. Swanson's particularly insightful observations and conclusions concerning the contribution of John Locke to American political unity and union. It should be confirmed, for the record, that she has made the life and writings of John Locke a focus of her time and labor and we trust that the refreshing and authoritative results of her research in this field will be published soon.

There are no accidents in His story and it is surely Providential that this *Study Guide* has been

v

completed at a time when American Christians need to understand not only when to separate but how to unite "when the fundamental principles of government or our holy religion are assaulted." (*Rudiments of America's Christian History and Government,* by Verna M. Hall and Rosalie J. Slater, "Letters to a Young Gentleman Commencing His Education" by Noah Webster, p. 7) Will we be compelled by political, economic and moral adversity to unite as Americans to preserve our civil and religious liberty, property and capacity for local self-government, or will we associate *voluntarily* as we remember the law of Love for God and our neighbor? May this *Study Guide,* together with Miss Hall's rich historic compilation, equip the reader with both the Biblical and practical expression of the principle of Christian Self-Government with Union.

James B. Rose
American Christian History Institute

INTRODUCTION

Since the publication of *The Christian History of the Constitution of the United States of America*, Volume I: *Christian Self-Government*, compiled by Verna M. Hall, many thoughtful readers have rejoiced in rediscovering their unique American Christian heritage as revealed in its pages. What they learned often confirmed deeply held convictions about the Christian foundations of our self-governing institutions. Its scholarly documentation helped teachers and students to understand (sometimes for the first time) the profound influence of Christianity upon our early Founding Fathers and upon the Framers of the United States Constitution.

Now, since the celebrations of the Bicentennial of the Constitution (1787–1791/1987–1991), there seems to be an increased desire to learn how our American union came into being and what our Founders intended to achieve in the unique national/federal system of government they gave us. There also appears to be a renewed desire to learn more about the *character* of the men who gave us our Constitution.

Finally, there is an awareness that if we are to hand down to the next generation the unique blessings of liberty, self-government and union that our forefathers bequeathed to us — and which they saw as the work of Divine Providence — we must understand the Christian origins of these blessings.

It is surely appropriate that during this Bicenten-nial period a *Study Guide* should at last appear for Volume II of the *Christian History of the Constitution* series — *Christian Self-Government with Union*, also compiled by Miss Hall, the Founder of the Foundation for American Christian Education in San Francisco. This rich collection of historical documents dealing with the development of American union extends the work she began in Volume I which dealt primarily with the development of self-government on the north American continent.

As Felix Morley explained in his Introduction to Volume II: "Although a unit in itself, Volume I was, in a sense, a preliminary compilation. Its documentation of the development of self-government begins with the Christian idea of the nature of man and terminates with the Declaration of Independence."

When, in 1965, Rosalie J. Slater wrote her book, *Teaching and Learning America's Christian History: The Principle Approach*, it added a new dimension to the usefulness of Miss Hall's compilation. In *Teaching and Learning*, Miss Slater used the historical materials in Volume I to teach students *seven fundamental principles* by which our forefathers lived. Her book also gave the reader two valuable courses for adults. (See *Teaching and Learning (T & L)*, p. 59 and p. 303)

In 1978, Rus Walton, President of Plymouth Rock Foundation, produced *Fundamentals for American Christians*, a Study Manual which documented Biblically some of the principles that were presented in Miss Slater's book. Mr. Walton emphasized the direct link that exists between Biblical principles and precepts and the individual American's liberty, self-government and right to hold property; the Bible as "the political textbook" of early Americans; and the need for American Christians today to restore and rebuild the republic's eroded foundations under God's guidance.

In 1981, the Mayflower Institute published *The American Covenant—the Untold Story* by Marshall Foster and Mary-Elaine Swanson which traced the covenantal roots of the Constitution, utilizing the historical documentation found in Volume I. The book dealt with several of the principles outlined in *Teaching and Learning — God's Principle of Individuality, the Christian Principle of Self-Government, "Conscience is the Most Sacred of all Property," and The Christian Form of our Government.* The goal of the authors was to prepare thousands of Americans to think more deeply about how the Hand of God and the truths of God's Word contributed to our early American character and our Constitution and to offer practical suggestions on how to restore the foundations of both the American character and the Constitution to their original Biblical basis.

The circulation of the books produced by Plymouth Rock Foundation and the Mayflower Institute have increasingly opened up new avenues for the study of Volume I and its companion book, *Teaching and Learning* — in Christian day schools, home schools and adult study groups in churches and homes.

Now, James B. Rose, President of the American Christian History Institute, has published his *Guide to American Christian Education,* as the fruitage of his many years of teaching the Principle Approach to parents and children, while Headmaster of the first Principle Approach school and later through his adult seminars and institutes. His book will enable parents and teachers to take hold of this unique teaching method predicated upon America's Christian history and government and put it to work in the home and the school.

Meanwhile, however, there has remained a rich vein of historical research in Volume II that has been largely untapped, but which is equally vital for Americans to understand before the original basis of our American union can be restored. As Felix Morley explained: "Now, Volume II carries this promising undertaking a stage farther. While its predecessor concentrated on the development of the idea and practise of self-government, this book is primarily concerned with the growth of the spirit of unity among Americans. It is a unity, the reader will soon discover, that is built from the ground up in the setting of Christian fellowship." (See Introduction, p. XXI)

Over the years since Vol. II first appeared in 1962, there have been suggestions that a Study Guide be produced enabling the student to explore its riches and apply its lessons to our time. It is perhaps providential that this has not happened until now. It has taken time for *Christian History,* Vol. I, to leaven and permeate the thinking of American Christians on the important *first lesson* our Founding Fathers had to learn (one which should be no less important to us today) — the principle of Christian Self-Government.

Those who have studied Vol. I understand that there is no better time than now, during these Bicentennial years, to study the *second important lesson* our Founding Fathers learned so well: *the Biblical balance between Christian self-government and union.* The United States of America was founded as a union that acknowledged and protected individual liberty and self-government under law. It also protected the integrity and independence of the individual states at the same time as it enabled them to act together cooperatively *for their general concerns.*

The Christian spirit of unity in defense of Christian self-government, as expressed in our early history, is beautifully documented in Vol. II. In its pages we learn that this spirit of unity enabled Americans to bring forth their unique national/federal union under the Constitution.

THE GOAL AND PURPOSE OF THIS STUDY GUIDE

The *goal* of the course outlined in this *Study Guide* is to equip the reader with a comprehensive understanding of the Christian foundations of the American system of government so that he may aid in reversing the trend of thinking among Americans from passive acquiescence in the divorce of religion from our constitutional heritage to an active defense and restoration of the Christian constitutional ideals of our forefathers. Scripture warns: "If the foundations be destroyed, what can the righteous do?" (Psalm 11:3) But may it not also be true that "If the foundations be restored, what can the unrighteous do?"

As Miss Hall observed in *The Christian History of the American Revolution: Consider and Ponder (C & P)* p. XXXV: "America from the days of creation has been for God's glory and for His people and if His people will be willing to learn what He has done for them in the days past, repent, and ask God's forgiveness for forgetting what He has done in bringing America into being, God will deal with her enemies within and without."

The *purpose* of this *Study Guide* is to focus on those selections under each heading in Volume II that show how and where our Founders discovered and developed the seeds of American unity and union. In the first half of the *Guide,* the student will explore such leading ideas as:

- The importance of "first principles" or "fundamental principles" to our Founding Fathers and how their political principles sprang from their Christian view of God, man and government. (See Lesson One)

- Our Founding Fathers' providential view of history and the westward movement of the Chain of Christianity. (Lesson Two)

- The Law of God revealed in Scripture and in His law of Nature written in men's hearts and discoverable through the God-given faculty of reason. (Lessons Three and Six)

- The Law of Nations as grounded in God's Law of Nature. (Lessons Three and Six)

- The contrast between the pagan and the Christian idea of man and government in ancient Greece and Rome. (Lesson Four)

- The need for the sanctity of law if it is to have power and authority in men's lives and the attempts of both the Roman Republic and the Roman Empire to found systems which would find their sanctity in human beings. (Lesson Five)

The second Half of the *Study Guide,* like the second half of Volume II, deals specifically with the development of American political union. The following topics, among others, are considered here:

- The leadership of the colonial clergy in educating the people to understand government from the Biblical perspective and how to stand up for their God-given rights in a constructive manner. (Lessons Eight and Nine)

- The importance to colonial Americans of the Stamp Act of 1765, Great Britain's first attempt to impose an internal tax on the colonists without their consent, and their response as seen in the political writings of Massachusetts patriots James Otis and Samuel Adams. (Lesson Eight)

- The tactics and methods of Christian resistance to British tyranny that were employed by the colonists during the decade of debate that began with the Stamp Act. (Lesson Nine)

- The importance of the individual's "life, liberty and property" as both a God-given and a con-

stitutional right, ably discussed by John Dickinson in his *Farmer's Papers.* (Lesson Ten)

- The Committees of Correspondence as one of the most effective methods for continental union and for educating the people in the principles that resolved the issues facing them. (Lesson Eleven)

- The Boston Tea Party as a proper action taken by the colonists to defend their legal rights under the English Constitution. (Lesson Eleven)

- The surprising effect of Great Britain's blockade of Boston in 1774—which united the colonies irrevocably in resistance to the Boston Port Bill as "unconstitutional in its principles and dangerous to the liberties of British America." It inspired an outpouring of Christian sympathy and support for Boston by the other colonies. "The noble record portrays the brotherhood that constituted the real union of the colonies. ... It is a Christian prologue grandly spoken on the entrance of the United Colonies into the family of nations." (Lesson Twelve)

- The fundamental principles stated in the Declaration of Rights and the other state papers of the first Continental Congress of 1774—papers that a great English statesman admired for their "solidity of reasoning and wisdom of conclusion" and that American statesman Daniel Webster later advised young men to master "and become imbued with their sentiments." (Lesson Twelve)

AMERICAN POLITICAL ACTION

The decade of debate (1765–1775) focused upon in the second half of the volume was a period when the colonists were asking themselves many questions pertaining to the natural and constitutional rights to their property, their local self-government, and their proper relationship with the Mother Country.

Through newspapers and pamphlets, many Americans participated directly in the great constitutional debate. As they educated themselves and grappled with the constitutional principles and issues that arose in their relationship with the Mother Country during this period, an extraordinary consensus slowly began to develop. By 1775, a genuine Christian unity of spirit had been achieved. (This period of constitutional debate is discussed in Lessons 8–12.)

A sample of the close reasoning and depth of historical documentation that appeared in many American pamphlets, is found in "The Rights of the British colonies Asserted and Proved,'' by James Otis, on pp. 370–391 of the text and in Lesson 8 of this *Guide*.

An example of the calibre of political writing in the newspapers of the time is an article written for the Boston Gazette by patriot leader Samuel Adams. It is found on pp. 469–474 of *Christian History*, Volume II, and is discussed in Lesson 11.

The tone of these pamphlets and newspaper articles reveals the American character as "profoundly reasonable,'' as historian Bernard Bailyn has written. These pamphleteers wanted to *persuade*, not destroy, their opponents. The colonists valued the Biblical injunction: "Come now, let us reason together, saith the Lord.'' (Isaiah 1:18)

This early American method of constitutional debate has much to teach Americans today. It enabled the colonists *to act constructively* in the face of British tyranny. Their publications contained an immense diversity of expression within a spirit of unity. This spirit of unity with diversity sprang from their Christianity and underlies American federalism.

Seven Important Questions

The first Lesson in this *Study Guide* is an overview of *Christian History*, Volume II, utilizing Miss Hall's *Preface* in which she asked seven important questions vital for today's American Christians to answer in order to preserve our Constitution and the civil and religious liberty it is intended to protect. (See *Preface*, p. II, and Lesson One of this *Study Guide* for Miss Hall's seven questions.)

It is hoped that this *Study Guide* will enable the student to arrive at the answers to all of these questions—and more—by the end of the course. The seven questions Miss Hall presents are, as she notes, the kinds of questions that American Christians of 200 years ago were well able to answer. Why were they so well equipped to answer them? Surely, it was because they had *learned from their pastors how to reason closely from Scripture on civil as well as ecclesiastical government*. They had learned to "think governmentally."

Study Method of This Guide

Pondering the best way to utilize the material in Volume II so that the student could gain the maximum benefits from the course, *i.e.*, how *to understand and apply* the principles of our forefathers to today's problems, the author has adapted the unique method Rosalie J. Slater introduced in her *Christian History Study Course* to Volume I, in *Teaching and Learning* (pp. 305–366).

Thus, the lessons in this Guide to Volume II progress through:

1) Study of the *fundamental principles* presented in each lesson.

   The over-arching principle, of the entire course, which should be kept in mind as the student pursues each lesson, is that the law of love—love for God and neighbour (Matthew 22:37–40)—is the foundation for the Christian principles of self-government and voluntary union that were worked out by our forefathers in their churches, communities, colonies, states and, finally, in a nation with its unique national/federal governmental system — the dual form of government.

2) Discussion of the *leading ideas* in the lesson that demonstrate the development of these principles in America with a Reading Assignment in *Christian History*, Vol. II, to identify the leading ideas.

3) *Questions for Invention*, based on the Reading Assignment in Step 2, are designed to help the student relate the lesson to his or her own life and to the conduct of our national life today.

4) *Further Study of Principles and Leading Ideas* is an optional step for those who wish to discover more about how these principles and ideas developed throughout history. The student should read the material in the *Study Guide* under Step Four of each lesson, even if further study under this section is omitted.

5) This step provides an opportunity for *original thought* by assigning an essay on the principles and leading ideas covered in the lesson.

6) Each lesson concludes with a *summary* of the principles and leading ideas in the lesson that are identified with the history of our American political union.

How the Study Guide May Be Used

This *Study Guide* may be used effectively by:

1. *The individual* for self-study,—*e.g.*, by the parent-teacher in the home or by the school teacher, by the businessman or woman or by the politician, by all who seek to understand better the roots of the American system of government.

2. *Adult Study Groups*. (See *Suggestions for Study Group Leaders*, p. XII)

3. After finishing this *Study Guide,* school teachers and home-schooling parents interested in teaching the Christian foundations of the Constitution to their pupils could adapt the material given under all six steps of the twelve lessons for a one-semester course for 11th and 12th graders on America's place on the Chain of Christianity from 50 A.D. to 1775.

A semester, or shorter, course, suitable for 10th–12th grades could also be given on the Formation of the American Union (1643–1775), covering roughly the second half of the text using Lessons Seven through Twelve, plus material in Lesson One on the terms "first principles" or "fundamental principles."

THE IMPORTANCE OF KEEPING A NOTEBOOK

Keeping a notebook is a most important adjunct to this *Study Guide* whether the study is being pursued by an individual on his or her own initiative, or as a member of a Study Group, or by a teacher or home-schooling parent and his pupils. A notebook provides a written record of the individual's understanding of the course. In the essays the student writes for each lesson, he will gain a mastery of the lesson material attainable in no other way. A study which otherwise might appear abstract and dry becomes vivid and challenging as one *internalizes* the principles and leading ideas through one's own study and then expresses them in written form with application to one's own life and to the life of the nation.

The importance of keeping notebooks — not just as a school child but throughout life — was not lost on our Founding Fathers who kept many notebooks, journals and diaries. John Adams repeatedly urged his son, John Quincy, to keep a journal. While with his father in Paris in 1778, John Quincy wrote to his mother: "My papa enjoins it upon me to keep a journal, or a diary of the events that happen to me, and of objects that I see, and of characters that I converse with from day to day.... My papa, who takes a great deal of pains to put me in the right way, has also advised me to keep copies of all my letters, and has given me a convenient blank book for this end; and altho' I shall have the mortification a few years hence to read a great deal of my childish nonsense, yet I shall have the pleasure and advantage of remarking the several steps by which I shall have advanced in taste, judgment, and knowledge." (See Rosalie J. Slater's "The Education of John Quincy Adams" in *Consider and Ponder,* p. 608)

In 1783, on John Quincy's return from service as secretary to the American minister to Russia, his father asked: "Have you kept a regular journal? If you have not, you will be likely to forget most of the observations you have made. If you have omitted this Useful Exercise, let me advise you to recommence it immediately."

The reasons Adams gave for keeping a travel journal are quite as pertinent to keeping a notebook for any course of study. He told John Quincy: "One contracts a Fondness for Writing by Use. We learn to write readily and what is of more importance, we think, and improve our Judgments, by committing our Thoughts to paper." (This interesting passage appears on page 349 of *The Book of Abigail and John, Selected Letters of the Adams Family 1762–1784,* published by the Harvard University Press in 1975.)

How rapidly this course is completed depends upon the amount of time and effort students are willing and able to give to the course. Whether progress is fast or slow on any journey, however, is less important than the sights and insights gained along the way. One often learns more about a country from a leisurely trip across its terrain than from one taken in such haste that there is no time to discover and savor its unique qualities. Similarly, it is good to take time to become thoroughly acquainted with our history and to remind ourselves:

"The more thoroughly a nation deals with its history, the more decidedly will it recognize and own an overruling Providence therein, and the more religious a nation will it become; while the more superficially it deals with its history, seeing only secondary causes and human agencies, the more irreligious will it be.... History is not a string of striking episodes, with no other connection but that of time. It is rather the working out of a mighty system, by means of regularly defined principles as old as creation, and as infallible as divine wisdom." (Rev. S. J. Foljambe, Boston, 1876, in *Consider and Ponder,* p. 46)

June 1988
Camarillo, California

Mary-Elaine Swanson

SUGGESTIONS
FOR STUDY GROUP
LEADERS

THE 24-WEEK STUDY PLAN

The best method for conducting this 12-lesson study course is to devote *two meetings* to each lesson. (An abbreviated 12-week study course is discussed on p. 15.)

In order to encourage discussion by all the students, the group should consist of no more than 15 persons.

Whether the meetings are held in the Study Group Leader's home, a church hall or a public meeting room, it would be helpful to have all the participants grouped around the same table, as this facilitates discussion.

If possible, the meetings should be for two to two-and-a-half hours, *e.g.,* from 7:00–9:00 or 9:30 in the evening or from 9:00 or 9:30 in the morning to 11:30 or 12:00 noon.

Meetings should not be scheduled too close together (because then the members may not have time to complete their assignments) or too far apart (because then interest lags and the members lose track of the date they are to meet). Meetings may be held every week, or every other week for 48 weeks if preferred.

The Leader may want to utilize a chalkboard from time to time, but should avoid lecturing, lest the participants sit back and wait to be "fed" instead of being actively engaged in reading the lesson and

reasoning from its contents. The Leader needs to help the participants to learn how to "4-R" the subject, *i.e.,* to learn how to research, reason, relate and record the lessons they are covering in this course. (See *Teaching and Learning America's Christian History (T&L)* by Rosalie J. Slater, pp. 88–89)

Each participant should have his own copy of this *Study Guide* and also of the text, *Christian Self-Government with Union (Union).* Other books that are helpful for the student to have are *Teaching and Learning America's Christian History (T&L),* by Miss Slater; *Christian History,* Vol. I, and *The Christian History of the American Revolution: Consider and Ponder* by Verna M. Hall; Noah Webster's *American Dictionary of the English Language* (1828); and *The Guide to American Christian Education,* by James B. Rose.

The *Study Guide* to Volume II by Mrs. Swanson and Mr. Rose's *Guide to American Christian Education* are available from:

American Christian History Institute,
P.O. Box 648,
Palo Cedro, CA 96073.

The other books may be ordered from:

Foundation for American Christian Education
Box 27035,
San Francisco, CA 94127.

FIRST MEETING:

As outlined briefly in the attached Chart, the Study Leader should begin the meeting with prayer, perhaps utilizing the Biblical quotation that begins the Lesson. The Leader should then explain the purpose of the course and the methodology that will be used. (See Lesson One for explanation and *T & L*, pp. 88–89)

After these introductory remarks, it would be helpful to ask the Study Group members to read aloud the introductory material for the Lesson on p. 1 and then under *Step One: Principles to Ponder*, pp. 2–3, stopping to discuss and clarify points as needed. If there are few comments or questions at first, stop and ask, "Are you all clear on this point?" For example, you may want to be sure that all participants understand the term "principle" as used in the text and why fundamental or "first principles" were so important to our Founding Fathers.

The need to understand what Christian self-government means and how to practice it needs to be brought out, as well as the importance of learning "how to live properly with one's neighbor." These are *major themes* of the text and will be seen in their many facets as they develop historically in the succeeding lessons.

At the first meeting, stress that it is important for all members of the study group to keep their own notebooks in which they will write their answers to the *Questions for Invention* in *Step Three* and their essay assignments from *Step Five*. (See the *Introduction* to this *Study Guide*, p. VII for a discussion on the importance of keeping a notebook.) Suggest that all participants in the study course get a sturdy 3-ring binder with 12 dividers, one for each lesson.

The first hour of the lesson will probably be needed to cover the introductory material and Step One of Lesson One. During the second hour, begin the discussion on *Step Two: Reading for Leading Ideas*. During this time, have the participants read directly from Miss Hall's *Preface* to *Union* and, if time permits, also read material on one of the pastors discussed in *T & L*, pp. 46–51. Explain that they are to complete their reading assignment in Step Two before the next meeting, and also complete *Step Three: Questions for Invention*.

SECOND MEETING:

During the first hour of the second meeting ask the participants to read aloud from their answers to Miss Hall's seven questions. (Because they should also answer and discusss the *Questions for Invention* during this hour, there may only be time to hear each student's answer to *one* of the questions. But, in the

other lessons, when there are only the questions from *Step Three* to answer, it would be good to hear from each student on all the questions. This will show the great diversity of expression that may exist among the members in their replies, yet each answer may be correct. Thus, the students will learn from each other's replies as well as from the Study Leader's comments. (An answer key to the Questions for Invention for each lesson is available to Study Group Leaders to help in evaluating the answers and, if desired, copies may be distributed to the group at the end of the meeting.)

During the second hour, the Study Group Leader may wish to discuss briefly the material in the optional step (*Step Four: Further Study of Principles and Leading Ideas*). This section is a short one in Lesson One, but is substantially longer in later lessons. It is good, however, to read aloud together the material for this section in the Study Guide, even though your Study Group elects not to do the additional reading and writing assignment in Step Four.

After reading Step Four in the *Study Guide* together and discussing it briefly, move on to the essay writing assignment in *Step Five: Original Thought*. Point out that in learning to write a good, short essay, they are preparing themselves to produce well-written letters for publication on the Editorial Page of their local newspapers — letters that not only express a personal opinion on a current governmental issue, but *document* it historically. This exercise of *Original Thought* also prepares them to write effective articles on America's Christian history for newspapers and magazines and to give effective talks before service organizations.

Before ending the meeting, refresh their understanding of how to write an essay, perhaps by using a chalkboard to define an essay's three parts: 1) the introduction of the subject; 2) the body of the article which develops the subject; and 3) the conclusion or conclusions drawn from the subject as introduced and developed in the essay.

A sample essay for Lesson One is available from the American Christian History Institute, along with an answer key to the questions used in each lesson, for the use of teachers and study group leaders.

During the second hour, if time permits, read over some of the key points of Philip Schaff's writing on the relationship between Church and State in America.

THIRD MEETING:

The members' essays on *The Historic Relationship Between Church and State in America* should be presented at this meeting. You may wish to have the participants read their essays aloud and discuss them, or you may prefer to collect the essays for return later with your comments. After reading (or collecting) the essays summarize Lesson One by going over *Step Six: What Christian Principles and Leading Ideas Identify the American Political Union?*

Then, begin Lesson Two with a discussion of the Chain of Christianity. Have the participants turn to p. 6 of the *Study Guide* and consult the chart reproduced from *Christian History,* Vol. I, on the Chain of Christianity. Ask them to turn to p. 1 of *Union* and have someone read Abraham Kuyper's quotation and the other quotations on pp. 1–2, which indicate what is to come under this opening section of the book.

Discuss God's Providence as the Chain of Christianity moved westward. Discuss also our forefather's providential view of history as seen in Rev. Foljambe's sermon, *The Hand of God in American History.*

Then have the study group read aloud and discuss the fundamental principles that will be unfolded in Lesson Two.

During the second hour, read together the material in the *Study Guide* for *Step Two: Reading for Leading Ideas* and perhaps one or two of the questions to be answered under *Step Three.*

FOURTH MEETING:

At this meeting Study Group Leaders should conclude Lesson Two by covering Steps Three, Four and Five as they did for Lesson One at the Second Meeting. (See the attached Chart for a quick outline of the systematic procedure for each lesson.)

Devoting two meetings to each lesson has proved to be the best way to assimilate the contents of this important volume at an easy pace. The method outlined here for Study Groups may be adapted for use in the school room.

THE 12-WEEK STUDY COURSE

This is an abbreviated study plan in which the Leader guides the group through an entire Lesson at each meeting, consisting of Steps One and Two: Principles to Ponder and Reading for Leading Ideas.

The Leader should select one question for each meeting from *Step Three* and give it to the Study Group participants at the beginning of the meeting, telling them that it is to be answered at the end of the session in a short essay. The only homework assignment is to read the material in *Union* under *Step Two: Reading for Leading Ideas.*

In this abbreviated plan, answering the *Questions for Invention* (Step Three) is omitted as are *Steps Four* and *Five.* This places a greater responsibility upon the Study Group Leader to summarize the other material in the lesson by utilizing the introductory passage at the beginning of each lesson and the summary in *Step Six.* It is suggested that the Leader also encourage the study group members to read through the material in the *Study Guide* under Steps Four and Five.

Because there is little homework involved in this abbreviated plan, it is possible to schedule a meeting each week, or every other week for 24 weeks if preferred. It is also true, however, that this abbreviated course, while useful, does not allow the student to gain as much in-depth knowledge of the subject or as much practice in writing as does the preferred 24-week Course.

SUGGESTED LESSON STRUCTURE
FOR 24-WEEK
STUDY GROUP PLAN

OUTLINE OF FIRST SIX MEETINGS

FIRST MEETING:

1. Discuss purpose of course and methodology (the 4-R's).*
2. Go through Preface to the text and discuss principles involved.
3. Ask students to answer the 7 questions at beginning of the Preface before starting on their homework.
4. Discuss students' homework to be done before the next lesson: A Reading Assignment (Step 2) and Questions for Invention (Step 3).

SECOND MEETING:

1. Discuss students' answers to Questions, Step 3 of Lesson One. (Collect for evaluation & return, or merely discuss a few replies at the meeting.)
2. Discuss homework assignment in Step 5, Original Thought.

THIRD MEETING

1. Essays to be turned in to Study Group Leader.
2. Review Lesson One (Step 6).
3. Begin Lesson Two. Discuss the Chain of Christianity.
4. Discuss the Principles of the lesson.
5. Read together from Step 2; Discuss homework assignment of Steps 2 & 3.

FOURTH MEETING:

1. Return essays on Lesson One and read one aloud.
2. Discuss answers to Questions for Lesson Two.
3. Discuss the homework assignment: Essay writing (Step 5 of Lesson Two).

FIFTH MEETING:

1. Collect essays.
2. Review Lesson Two.
3. Begin Lesson Three. Discuss Principles and Leading Ideas of lesson.
4. Discuss homework assignment of Steps 2 & 3.

SIXTH MEETING:

1. Return essays on Lesson Two and read one.
2. Discuss answers to Questions for Lesson Three.
3. Discuss the homework assignment: Essay writing, in Step 5 of Lesson Three.

*See *Guide*, Lesson One; and *T & L*, pp. 88–89.

CHRISTIAN UNITY: THE BASIS OF THE AMERICAN UNION

Thou shalt love the Lord thy God with all thy heart, and with all thy soul, and with all thy mind.
This is the first and great commandment. And the second is like unto it, Thou shalt love thy neighbour as thyself.
On these two commandments hang all the law and the prophets. (Matthew 22:37–40)

Before beginning the lesson, be sure to read the *Introduction* to this *Study Guide* which explains the purpose of the *Guide* and how to use it. Then turn to the *Preface* of your text, *Christian History of the Constitution*, Volume 2: *Christian Self-Government with Union*, which will be referred to in this *Guide* as *Union* or simply as "your text." Note the seven questions that constitute paragraph 2 on page II. Write these questions in your notebook and answer them as well as you can without reading any further in the text. (At the end of Lesson 12, you will be asked to answer these questions again in the light of what you have learned and then compare your answers with those you gave in this lesson.)

- How does Christianity influence mankind's desire and ability to voluntarily cooperate or work together?

- Do the Biblical precepts relating to individuals working together, or simply getting along with one another, apply also to nations?

- Or, is there one set of rules for the individual and another for the state or nation?

- Is voluntary union among men and nations possible, or must joint actions be accomplished through law and force?

- Must large scale operations among men and nations be accomplished solely through fiat, edict, national government or international organizations backed by armed force, or can they be accomplished through voluntary means?

- Is voluntary cooperation only to be used at the local level, or can it be effective over larger geographic areas?

- Does time, or rapid communications, or increased population, or diversity of races and creeds affect voluntary cooperation?

In studying Lesson One and those that follow, you will be following six steps designed to help you develop an understanding of the *principles* presented and their *historical outworking*. These steps are also intended to help you relate these studies to your own life and the life of our nation today. It is hoped that these six steps will not only help develop your ability to *research, reason,* and *relate* these fundamental principles to your own life, but will enable you to *record* them in written form in *your own words* thus making the principles discussed your own and enabling you to instruct others in the history of American Christian self-government with union. (See Rosalie J. Slater, *Teaching and Learning America's Christian History: The Principle Approach (T & L)*, pp. 88–89)

STEP ONE:
PRINCIPLES TO PONDER

According to Noah Webster's 1828 *American Dictionary of the English Language*, the word *principle* is derived from the Latin *principium*, meaning beginning. Webster's definition reads (in part):

"1. In *a general sense*, the cause, source or origin of any thing; that from which a thing proceeds; as the *principle of motion*; the *principles* of action.

"3. Being that produces any thing; operative cause . . .

"5. Ground; foundation; that which supports an assertion, an action, or a series of actions or of reasoning . . .

"6. A general truth; a law comprehending many subordinate truths; as the principles of morality, of law, of government, etc."

Our Founding Fathers' understanding of the word "principle" falls into two categories:

1. As "the cause, source or origin of any thing," its "ground or foundation," which, in the most fundamental sense of the word, refers to God and His Word, for "other foundations no man can lay than that is laid." (I Corinthians 3:11)

2. As "a general truth, a law comprehending many subordinate truths; as the principles of morality, of law, of government." They found the origin for these general truths or principles of all things in God's Law in the Bible or His law written in men's hearts and confirmed by the Scriptures. Hence, their political principles were derived from God's laws.

The principles in Step One of each of the following lessons fall into either the first or the second category: God's laws and His Biblical principles or those principles of the social, legal, and political realm that the Founders derived from His laws. For example, the Founding Fathers only accepted as principles of morality those rules which accorded with or proceeded from the moral law in the Scriptures and not merely from men's invention. Their principles of law were rooted and grounded in the Scriptures, as is evident in the writings of William Blackstone which they studied assiduously. Finally, their principles of ecclesiastical and civil government were derived from their Christian view of God and man.

Since this *Guide* deals with the development of our constitutional system of government, the larger number of quotations under *Principles to Ponder* may consist of these secondary political or governmental principles. But the student should keep in mind the *ground or foundation*, the *source and origin* implicit in these principles. Without the Bible and the Biblical view of man and government, the founders of our nation would never have arrived at the inspired political principles they gave to us.

Foremost among their political principles was the conviction that men's rights to "life, liberty and property" were bestowed by God, not men, and that *both* religious and civil liberty were the gift of God. The Virginia Declaration of Rights of May 1776 warns "that no free Government, or the blessing of liberty, can be preserved to any people but by a firm adherence to justice, moderation, temperance, frugality, and virtue, and by frequent recurrence to *fundamental principles*. (The Massachusetts Declaration of Rights of 1780 reiterates this reliance on "a frequent recurrence to fundamental principles.")

The Virginia Declaration identifies some of these "fundamental principles": "That all men are by nature equally free and independent, and have certain inherent rights, of which, when they enter into a state of society, they cannot, by any compact, deprive or divest their posterity; namely, the enjoyment of life and liberty, with the means of acquiring and possessing property, and pursuing and obtaining happiness and safety."

Other "fundamental principles" follow: "That Government is, or ought to be, instituted for the common benefit, protection and security of the people, nation or community . . . ." and "That Religion, or the duty which we owe to our *Creator* . . . can be directed only by reason and conviction, not by force or violence; and, therefore, all men are equally entitled to the free exercise of religion, according to the dictates of conscience; and that it is the mutual duty of all to practise Christian forebearance, love and charity, towards each other."

THE PRINCIPLE OF PRINCIPLES

The Founding Fathers often referred to "fundamental principles" or "first principles." Many of the political principles of the Founding Fathers will be studied in this course as they pertain to the achievement of our unique political system which embraces both Christian self-government and Biblical Christian unity. *The most important principle behind all of the Founding Fathers' political principles is to be found in Matthew 22:37–40.*

In her *Preface*, Miss Hall introduces this fundamental principle and shows how it developed in America to produce:

• Voluntary cooperation between individuals to form churches.

- Voluntary union at the local level to form communities, then colonies and, subsequently, states.

- Voluntary union at the national level, beginning with the Committees of Correspondence of 1774, two years before the Declaration of Independence.

Miss Hall comments that "Never in the history of the world has there been such an example of Christian voluntary union in civil affairs as was exhibited by the colonists between 1775 and 1783" and that this "laid the groundwork for the adoption of our National Federal Constitution six years later in 1789." (*Union*, p. III)

In keeping with Matthew 22:37–40, Miss Hall also points out that there are *two lessons* American Christians need to learn in order to "successfully develop, maintain or restore" our republic:

- The first is Christian self-government

- The second is learning "how to live properly with one's neighbor."

STEP TWO:
READING FOR LEADING IDEAS

The purpose of this step is to trace *how* fundamental principles were developed in our nation. What were the leading ideas that developed these principles in America? The leading idea of this lesson is well expressed by Miss Hall's words on page V of the text:

"... the American idea of union is unique to the world, and came about through the leadership of the clergy and the responsiveness of the citizenry as they learned to live the two commandments of our Lord."

THE LEADERSHIP OF THE CLERGY

One pastor's explanation of what it means to love God and one's neighbor as oneself appears on page III. As Dr. Sewall's sermon was meant to be heard, try reading the excerpts aloud to yourself pondering their meaning. Consider that he was but one of many colonial pastors who educated their congregations well in Biblical principles of government over a period of some 150 years.

Consult the biographical notes on four of these pastors in *T & L*, pp. 46–51. Each pastor was a distinct individual who addressed himself to different problems facing civil government, but all four men shared a deep love for Christian self-government and the unity of Christians in defense of rights they deemed to be God-given.

THE DISTINCTIVE CHARACTER OF AMERICAN CHRISTIANITY

Philip Schaff's definition of the *distinctive character* of American Christianity (in *Church and State in the United States*), is striking:

"It is a free church in a free state, or a self-supporting Christianity in independent but friendly relations to the civil government."

Now, before proceeding to Step Three, read the *Preface* to your text (pp. II–VI). Then read the extracts from Philip Schaff on pp. 35–40.

STEP THREE:
QUESTIONS FOR INVENTION

Rosalie J. Slater explains her use of the word invention for this section of her Study Course for *Christian History*, Volume 1:

"Part of the Webster, 1856 definition of the word 'invention' is 'To find out something new.' An aspect of invention is *devise* and this word is defined in part as 'to *think*, divide or share, to *talk* or *interchange thoughts.*' A further aspect of *invent* is to *contrive* or by definition, 'to form *principles*, or *new arrangements of ideas, new applications of principles, or new arrangements of parts.*'"

The questions in this lesson are designed to help you apply the principles of Christian self-government and voluntary Christian unity taught by early American pastors, as seen in this lesson, to your life and the life of our nation today. (Be sure to write the questions with your answers in your notebook.)

1. What is the law our Lord gives us for living together in harmony?

2. Why is civil liberty dependent upon Christian self-government? (See Felix Morley's comments on p. XXIII)

3. What is the alternative to voluntary union?

4. Why is Christian character essential to the preservation of our republic?

5. What is the duty of the church in relation to the republic?

6. Does civil government in our republic have a duty to the churches?

7. Why are republican institutions in the hands of a corrupt and irreligious people the most effective means of destroying liberty and republican government itself?

8. If an *individual's* efforts to be self-governing are modeled on changing, mutable standards, not on God's laws, what is likely to result? Can you think of some examples from your personal observation or experience?

9. If a *society's* efforts to be self-governing are modeled on changing, mutable standards, what will be the result? What did Jesus have to say about this kind of building?

10. What good effects on our society might come about if the history courses in the public schools once again taught children the *role of religion* in early American life — the faith of the Pilgrim Fathers; the founding of their communities on the basis of covenanting together, as they did in their churches; the profound faith in Divine Providence of the leaders of the American Revolution and the framers of the United States Constitution?

Step Four:
Further Study of Principles and Leading Ideas

This step is designed for the student who wants to take more time for further study of the fundamental principles and leading ideas of each lesson. For this lesson, read Felix Morley's *Introduction* to the text. Consider his statement: "Union, when built from below by mutual faith, is natural and solid. Union, when dictated from above by arbitrary command, is artificial and brittle." Does this not suggest the importance of the *voluntary principle* and government by *consent of the governed?*

Why do you suppose Morley refers to the natural condition of man as slavery? Where does slavery begin? What sets men free from slavery? What is the first pre-requisite for freedom in the political sense?

If you wish, write your thoughts on these questions and others discussed in Morley's *Introduction* in a short one- or two-page essay.

Step Five:
Original Thought

Miss Slater said of the step in her Study Course (for Vol. 1) devoted to Original Thought: "This step

is designed to challenge some original response to the principles and ideas focused in the lesson and to enable each individual to relate America's *Christian History* to himself." (See Rosalie J. Slater, *T & L*, p. 305)

The vehicle for the student's original thought is essay writing on a suggested topic with specific questions to answer in the essay and directed reading on the subject.

The Reading Assignment for Step Five is to re-read Prof. Schaff's remarks on American Christianity in your text, pp. 35–40. After reading it again, *write a short essay* on the relationship between church and state in America as conceived by our Founding Fathers and as understood by the men of Philip Schaff's day.

In your essay, consider the following questions: Was this relationship an adversarial one, or a friendly, mutually supportive one? Upon what does "the American separation of church and state" rest? How does this kind of separation differ from "the infidel theory" of separation? What were the results of "the infidel theory" of separation when it was tried during the French Revolution of 1789? (See pp. 39–40) Does the first amendment to the Constitution imply freedom *from* religion or freedom *in* religion?

To assist you further in your writing assignment, here are some excerpts on the meaning of the First Amendment, from *The American Covenant — The Untold Story* by Marshall Foster and Mary-Elaine Swanson:

"The term 'separation of church and state' is used today as a catch-all phrase to eliminate religious influence upon anything involving the state or civil affairs. The history of the First Amendment to the Constitution gives us quite a different perspective. Our Founders had come from European lands ruled by monarchies which used official state churches to control the people. They had had enough of the supposed 'divine right of kings.' So, according to James Madison, the First Amendment was drawn up because "the people feared one sect might obtain pre-eminence, or two combine together, and establish a religion to which they would compel others to conform." The amendment was meant to shield the churches from the encroachment of the Federal Government, specifically, the Congress. But the framers of the Bill of Rights never intended that the church (speaking of the Christians and their various denominations) was to have no influence over the state. . . .

". . . it is well to remind ourselves of what the First Amendment actually says: 'Congress shall make no law respecting an establishment of religion, or prohibiting the free exercise thereof . . . ' John W. Whitehead, a respected Constitutional lawyer and author, gives the following excellent paraphrase of the Amendment into modern English: 'The federal government shall make no law having anything to do with supporting a national denominational church, or prohibiting the free exercise of religion.' (*The American Covenant*, pp. 7–8)

STEP SIX:

WHAT CHRISTIAN PRINCIPLES AND IDEAS IDENTIFY THE AMERICAN POLITICAL UNION?

This step summarizes the particular Christian principles and leading ideas discussed in the lesson in their historical context. This lesson revealed that:

- Americans learned to be self-governing in accord with Christ's Two Commandments before they could achieve voluntary union as independent states and then union as one people under the Constitution (See *Union*, p. III)

- American Christians worked out the Christian principle of voluntary union as a new alternative to the age-old compulsory union that existed under kings and emperors. (See *Union*, p. II)

- Leading the people in the development of Christian self-government with union were the colonial clergy. (*Union*, pp. III–IV; see also extracts from colonial sermons in *Christian History*, Volume 1, pp. 372–390)

   "Those who led in the church, and those who led in the field, were impelled by one conviction and labored together with the same design. One taught the law of justice, the other defended it; one was the voice of God, the other was His arm. Thus, the American Colonies, confederated by patriotism and piety long before they were united under a written Constitution, felt that their resistance to oppression was a common cause . . . ." (E. L. Magoon, "Orators of the American Revolution," in *Teaching and Learning*, p. 46)

- The Framers of the Constitution intended freedom IN religion, not freedom FROM religion. (See your text, Philip Schaff, on *American Christianity*, p. 40)

   As late as 1835, the distinguished French observer, Alexis De Tocqueville, wrote, "Religion in America takes no direct part in the government of society, but it must be regarded as the first of their political institutions; for if it does not impart a taste for freedom, it facilitates the use of it. . . . I do not know whether all Americans have a sincere faith in their religion — for who can search the human heart? — but I am certain that they hold it to be indispensable to the maintenance of republican institutions. This opinion is not peculiar to a class of citizens or to a party, but it belongs to the whole nation and to every rank of society." (See *Democracy in America*, Vol. 1, p. 316, in Vintage Books Edition, New York, 1955)

- The Founding Fathers did indeed find their inspiration for their union under state constitutions and then the United States Constitution in the Two Commandments of our Lord. This is seen in the writings of John Adams who greatly admired "A Short Treatise of Politicke Power" written by the 16th century English cleric, Rev. John Ponet. Adams said that it contained "all the essential principles of liberty."

   Ponet wrote that the Law that should govern nations as well as individuals was found in the Ten Commandments which were "reduced by Christ our saveour into these two wordes: Thou shalt love thy lorde God above all things, and thy neighbor as thyself. The latter part whereof he also expoundeth. What so ever ye will that men doo unto you, doo ye even so to them. In this lawe is comprehended all justice, the perfit way to serve and glorifie God, and the right meane to rule every man particularly, and all men generally: and the only staye to mayntayne every commonwealth." (*Union*, p. 140)

   Adams also called "the general principles of Christianity: and the general principles of English and American Liberty" *fundamentals* for American education. (Cited by Page Smith in *The Shaping of America*, p. 359)

5

CHAIN OF CHRISTIANITY MOVES WESTWARD
WITH "SIGNS FOLLOWING"

Note: This list of names, events, and nations is not intended to be exhaustive, but rather indicative of the fact that God used men and nations through Christ to bring forth America and her form of government, for His glory and for all the nations of the earth.

"RELIGION STANDS ON TIP-TOE IN OUR LAND, READIE TO PASS TO THE AMERICAN STRAND."
—George Herbert

HENRY HELWYS 1612
JOHN MILTON 1608
RICHARD MATHER 1596
WILLIAM BRADFORD 1590
JOHN WINTHROP 1588
THOMAS HOOKER 1586
HUGO GROTIUS 1583
JOHN ROBINSON 1575
WILLIAM BREWSTER 1563
GENEVA BIBLE 1557
PRELUDE TO AMERICA

RICHARD HOOKER 1554?
GASPARD DE COLIGNY 1519
JOHN FOX 1516
JOHN CALVIN 1509
JOHN KNOX 1505?
WILLIAM TYNDALE 1494
MILES COVERDALE 1488
HUGH LATIMER 1485
ULRICH ZWINGLI 1484
MARTIN LUTHER 1483
JOHANN GUTENBERG 1396
JOHN HUSS 1369
WYCLIFFE 1324?
MORNING STARS OF REFORMATION

MAGNA CHARTA 1215

IRELAND—PATRICK 389
AUGUSTINE 354
JEROME 340
FOURTH CENTURY

GERMANY
BRITAIN
SPAIN
FRANCE—FRANKS (GAUL)
SECOND CENTURY

ROME
GREECE
EUROPE—LYDIA (ACTS 16)
FIRST WESTWARD PLANTING OF SEEDS OF CHRISTIANITY
FIRST CENTURY

APOSTLES AND DISCIPLES
PAUL'S MISSIONARY JOURNEYS

JESUS CHRIST AND
GOSPEL—GRACE
MOSES AND TEN
COMMANDMENTS—LAW

AMERICA'S PLANTING
JAMESTOWN 1607
KING JAMES BIBLE 1611
MAYFLOWER COMPACT 1620

PILGRIMS LAND AT PLYMOUTH 1620
PETITION OF RIGHT 1628
JOHN BUNYAN 1628

WILLIAM PENN 1644
BILL OF RIGHTS 1689
LOCKE'S TREATISE ON GOVERNMENT 1689

GEORGE WHITEFIELD 1714
MONTESQUIEU 'THE SPIRIT OF LAWS' 1748
BLACKSTONE'S "COMMENTARIES" 1765

CHRISTOPHER DOCK 1698
JONATHAN EDWARDS 1703
JOHN AND CHARLES WESLEY 1703, 1707

THE DECLARATION OF INDEPENDENCE 1776

A NEW NATION
THE CONSTITUTION OF THE UNITED STATES OF AMERICA 1787

NINETEENTH CENTURY
THE MONROE DOCTRINE 1823

"ITS WESTERN COURSE THROUGH CHINA AND JAPAN IS IMPEDED . . . BY MODERNISM."
—Abraham Kuyper, 1898, Princeton

WESTWARD THE COURSE OF EMPIRE
"WESTWARD THE COURSE OF EMPIRE TAKES ITS WAY, THE FIRST FOUR ACTS ALREADY PAST, A FIFTH SHALL CLOSE THE DRAMA WITH THE DAY; TIME'S NOBLEST OFFSPRING IS THE LAST."
— Berkeley

6

LESSON TWO

THE SPIRIT OF AMERICAN UNITY AT HOME AND ABROAD

If you love me, keep my commandments.
(John 14:15)

As a prelude to this lesson, let us first consider America's place in the westward movement of Christianity. A provocative quotation from Abraham Kuyper on page 1 of your text describes this westward movement:

"There is but one world-stream, broad and fresh, which from the beginning bore the promise of the future. This stream had its rise in Middle Asia and the Levant, and has steadily continued its course from East to West.... From Greece it passed on to the Roman Empire. From the Romanic nations it continued its way to the Northwestern parts of Europe, and from Holland and England it reached at length your continent... the course of this world-stream from East to West can be denied by none."

THE CHAIN OF CHRISTIANITY MOVES WESTWARD

The political expression of Christian unity, which finally flowered in America, developed providentially as the Christian idea of man and government moved Westward on the Chain of Christianity. Consider the chart on the facing page (reproduced from page 6A of *The Christian History of the Constitution*, Vol. I). Note that the westward movement of Christianity began when the Apostle Paul responded to the vision of the man from Macedonia calling him to "come over and help us." As a result of this God-sent vision, Paul took Christianity into Europe beginning with his establishment of the first European church at Philippi in the home of his first European convert, Lydia, "the seller of purple." (See Acts 16)

Note, too, how many important links on this chain were forged before it extended to the New World. As Rosalie J. Slater points out (*T & L*, p. 312): "Each link of Christianity's Chain... promoted the Christian idea of man and government as Christianity moved westward."

We should remember that each step in the development of the Christian idea of man and government, as it providentially moved westward, required the *courage* and *constancy* of Christians that is implied in John 14:15 quoted above. It required, for example, the courage and constancy of Archbishop Stephen Langton who urged the Magna Charta on a reluctant monarch; of Wycliffe and Tyndale who gave the Bible to Englishmen in their own tongue that they might be governed by God's Holy Word; of the great reformers, Luther and Calvin, who taught men the importance of faith and the sovereignty of God; of the Pilgrim Fathers who brought their Biblical view of church government to bear upon their "civil body politick" in the Mayflower Compact; of our Founding Fathers who believed that the rights of men were God given and who, with "a firm reliance on the protection of divine Providence" pledged their lives,

7

fortunes and sacred honor to each other in the Declaration of Independence; of the Framers of the Constitution who, against seemingly insuperable odds, secured "a more perfect union" under the Constitution.

In a remarkable sermon, *The Hand of God in History* (1876), Rev. S. W. Foljambe referred to such men as "God's gift to the world, [who] in their thought and work indicate the world's progress and are its means and helpers." (See *The Christian History of the American Revolution: Consider and Ponder*, by Verna M. Hall, p. 48) Rev. Foljambe saw God's hand throughout history in the men He raised up for the times. "He who makes the times go over us, has always the men ready to meet them." (*Consider and Ponder*, p. 52)

Let us now learn how the men God provided for America worked out their political union. This lesson considers: 1) How Christianity, when planted *internally* in the hearts and minds of Americans, produced *externally* a uniquely American concept of liberty and union which was finally embodied in the United States Constitution; and 2) How the Founding Fathers developed the political principles that were to govern the relations of the United States with other nations.

STEP ONE:
PRINCIPLES TO PONDER

1. THE PRINCIPLE OF CHRISTIAN LOVE

"He gives them (the disciples) a bond of union, by which they should always be linked to Him and to each other in the principle of love.... The apologists of the first centuries delighted in appealing to the striking fact of the common love of Christians, which was a new thing in the history of mankind. ... By their love for each other, for mankind, for God, is it known or denied that men who call themselves Christians are really Christ's disciples." (W. H. Watkins, *Union*, p. 2)

"Our Saviour's great rule, that 'we should love our neighbor as ourselves,' is such a fundamental truth for the regulating of human society, that, by that alone, one might without difficulty determine all the cases and doubts in social morality." (John Locke, *Union*, p. 16)

"The sum of it is wonderful for its substantial brevity; that we should love God above all things, and our neighbour as ourselves; that is, we should do to others as we would have them do to us." (Hugo Grotius, *Union*, p. 16)

2. THE PRINCIPLE OF CHRISTIAN LIBERTY DISPLACES THE ANCIENT CENTRALIZATION

"The ancient centralization . . . had fallen before the principle which it had for ages overpowered. This was the liberty of the subject as well as the ruler who recognizes his responsibilities to his fellow-creatures and to his Creator.... It was the liberty to live according to the law of love proclaimed by Christ the Lord.... This was the appointed work of the early Christians. They were to prepare the union one day destined to take the place of the ancient centralization." (Samuel Eliot, "History of Liberty" (1853), *Union*, p. 2)

3. THE LAW OF NATIONS

"If all nations would submit to the law of Christ, and live up to it, whereunto there should nothing be wanting on God's Part; for it is certain, if all were Christians, and lived like Christians, there would be no wars...." (Hugo Grotius, *Union*, p. 19)

"The rules of international morality . . . are founded on the supposition, that the conduct which is observed by one nation towards another, in conformity with these rules, will be reciprocally observed by other nations towards it." (Henry Wheaton, *Union*, p. 23

"That international law, common to all civilized and Christian nations, which our ancestors brought with them from Europe, and which was obligatory upon us whilst we continued to form a part of the British Empire, did not cease to be so when we declared our independence of the parent country." (Henry Wheaton, *Union*, p. 23)

"The Unity of government which constitutes you one people is also now dear to you. It is justly so, for it is a main pillar in the edifice of your real independence.... Observe good faith and justice toward all nations. Cultivate peace and harmony with all. Religion and morality enjoin this conduct." (George Washington, *Union*, pp. 27–28)

4. THE MONROE DOCTRINE DEFENDS THE PRINCIPLE OF LOCAL SELF-GOVERNMENT

"The occasion has been judged proper for asserting, as a principle in which the rights and interests of the United States are involved that the American continents, by the free independent condition which they have assumed and maintain, are henceforth not to be considered as subjects for future colonization by any European powers.... We should consider any attempt on their part to extend their system to any portion of this hemisphere as dangerous to our peace and safety." (James Monroe, *Union*, pp. 31-32)

STEP TWO:
READING FOR LEADING IDEAS

You have two Reading Assignments for Step Two of this lesson: one relating to America's unity as a nation; and the other pertaining to the American union in relation to other nations.

AMERICAN NATIONAL UNITY
AS SEEN BY DANIEL WEBSTER

Your first Reading Assignment is the extracts from Daniel Webster's July 4th Oration on pages 4–12. Since these words were meant to be spoken, you might want to read the extracts aloud and see if this does not help make their meaning clearer and more vivid.

In his Oration, this great American statesman and orator speaks of the unique character of American liberty, showing how it differed from the ideas of liberty held by the Greeks and the Romans. He outlines four important American political principles and three necessary character qualities for the preservation of these principles in our government. (*Union*, pp. 6–8)

AMERICAN FOREIGN RELATIONS

Your second Reading Assignment is found on pages 24–32, under *American Foreign Relations*. It deals with three important American documents which have had a profound effect on the conduct of American foreign policy and whose wisdom should be heeded today if we wish to preserve the blessings of liberty to our posterity.

1. *The Declaration of Independence* was a clear statement of the principles on which we proposed to found a new nation. In severing their connection with Great Britain and becoming "free and independent states" the former colonies became a nation. In the opening sentence of the Declaration of Independence they declared the necessity of assuming a "separate and equal Station to which the Laws of Nature and Nature's God entitle them...." This new status as a nation presupposed not only a set of political principles to rule "the United States in Congress Assembled" but also the development of political principles for the guidance of the new nation in its relations with the other nations of the world.

2. *Washington's Farewell Address* warned of the dangers of involvement in the political affairs of other nations. His counsel is still timely:

"... it must be unwise in us to implicate ourselves by artificial ties in the ordinary vicissitudes of [European] politics or the ordinary combinations and collisions of her friendships or enmities." (*Union*, p. 29)

Washington pointed out that "it is folly in one nation to look for disinterested favors from another; that it must pay with a portion of its independence ..." and that "There can be no greater error than to expect or calculate upon real favors from nation to nation." (*Union*, p. 30)

3. *The Monroe Doctrine*. Under President James Monroe, American foreign policy became one of non-intervention in the affairs of other nations. Even as we valued our independence as a nation, we respected the right to independence of other nations. Note Monroe's remarks on page 31 of your text:

"The citizens of the United States cherish sentiments the most friendly in favor of the liberty and happiness of their fellow-men on that side of the Atlantic. In the wars of the European powers in matters relating to themselves we have never taken any part, nor does it comport with our policy so to do.

"It is only when our rights are invaded or seriously menaced," he continues, "that we resent injuries or make preparation for our defense. With the movements in this hemisphere we are of necessity more immediately connected, and by causes which must be obvious to all enlightened and impartial observers."

In his statement of America's foreign policy, note that Monroe went on to explain we would not interfere with any existing colonies European powers had in South America, but any meddling with the governments in that region that had declared their independence would be opposed. He declared that "...we could not view any interposition for the purpose of oppressing them, or controlling in any other manner their destiny, by any European power in any other light than as the manifestation of an unfriendly disposition toward the United States...." (*Union*, p. 32)

President Monroe, and John Quincy Adams, his Secretary of State, correctly saw also that "It is impossible that the allied powers should extend their political system to any portion of either continent without endangering our peace and happiness; nor can anyone believe that our southern brethren, if left to themselves, would adopt it of their own accord." (*Ibid.*) Do not their words still hold true today?

Step Three:
Questions for Invention

1. Daniel Webster writes of our American inheritance of liberty as uniquely our own. How did it differ from either Grecian or Roman liberty? (See *Union*, pp. 6–7)

2. Webster states that the principles of American liberty were so "interwoven" in the minds of Americans of his day that wherever an American goes he takes with him "fully developed in his own understanding and experience our American principles... and becomes ready at once, in cooperation with others, to apply them to the formation of new governments...." (See *Union*, p. 7) Do you think this is still true today? If so, why? If not, why not?

3. What are the four unique American political principles that Daniel Webster describes and why is it important to understand them today? (*Union*, p. 7)

4. Today the American system is often described as a democracy in which the will of the majority rules. What two vital principles of our Founding Fathers are *omitted* from this definition?

5. What does Webster give as the three key elements that must support "a useful and wise government" based on our unique American principles? Have these three elements become seriously eroded? If so, what can be done to restore them? (*Union*, p. 8)

6. What produces virtue in an individual and in a nation? Can you separate the two, *i.e.*, is it likely that a man who has a low standard of personal morality will be a moral public servant?

7. What were the truths that our Founding Fathers pronounced "self-evident" in the Declaration of Independence? (See *Union*, p. 25)

8. What kind of conduct did George Washington say America ought to maintain toward other nations? (*Union*, p. 28)

9. Washington counseled against either a "persistent antipathy" toward some nations or a "passionate attachment" for others. What were his reasons for these views? Do you think he would favor the custom today of according "most favored nation" status to some countries with which we trade and not to others? If not, why do you think he would oppose such a policy?

10. Why does the Monroe Doctrine state "as a principle" that "the American continents... are henceforth not to be considered as subjects for future colonization by any European powers"? What did President James Monroe and his Secretary of State, John Quincy Adams (who drafted the doctrine), fear would happen if European powers began to colonize in our hemisphere? (See *Union*, p. 32) Can we see evidence today of the reasonableness of these fears?

STEP FOUR:
FURTHER STUDY OF PRINCIPLES AND LEADING IDEAS

Those students who have the time to do so should study the selections on the Law of Nations in *Union*, on pp. 19–24. Note Henry Wheaton's comments on p. 20: "The introduction of Christianity tended to abolish the Pagan precept: 'Thou shalt hate thine enemy,' and to substitute for it the benevolent command: 'Love your enemies,' which could not be reconciled with perpetual hostility between the different races of men.... During the Middle Ages the Christian States of Europe began to unite, and to acknowledge the obligation of an international law common to all who professed the same religious faith...."

THE GREAT JURISTS OF THE REFORMATION

The Reformation pushed forward the idea of a Law of Nations through the writings of such great Protestant jurists as Hugo Grotius and others (whose writings you will study in Lesson Six).

"The rules of international morality recognized by these writers are founded on the supposition, that the conduct which is observed by one nation towards another, in conformity with these rules, will be reciprocally observed by other nations towards it. The duties which are imposed by these rules are enforced by moral sanctions, by apprehension on the part of sovereigns and nations of incurring the hostility of other States, in case they should violate maxims generally received and respected by the civilized world. ..." (*Union*, p. 23)

Wheaton makes the important point that the Law of Nations "common to all civilized and Christian nations, which our ancestors brought with them from Europe, and which was obligatory upon us whilst we continued to form a part of the British Empire, did not cease to be so when we declared our independence of the parent country. Its obligation was acknowledged by the Continental congress, in the

10

ordinances published by that illustrious assembly for the regulation of maritime captures, and by the Court of Appeals, established for the adjudication of prize causes during the War of the Revolution. In the mean time, the United States had recognized, in their treaty of alliance with France, those principles respecting the rights of neutral commerce and navigation which subsequently became the basis of the armed neutrality of the northern powers of Europe." (*Union*, pp. 23–24)

Conforming to the Principles of Eternal Justice

Early on, the government of the United States recognized that its foreign policy must conform to "the Law of Nations" which, in turn, was founded on "the principles of eternal justice" to which Wheaton refers, quoting British statesman, Edmund Burke: "Justice is the great standing policy of civil society, and any eminent departure from it, under any circumstances, lies under the suspicion of being no policy at all." (*Union*, p. 21)

Note also John W. Foster's observations in your text (p. 24) that our nation, "from the beginning of its political existence . . . made itself the champion of a freer commerce, of a sincere and genuine neutrality, of respect for private property in war, of the most advanced ideas of natural rights and justice . . . by its example and its persistent diplomatic advocacy, it has exerted a greater influence in the recognition of these elevated principles than any other nation of the world."

After reading these selections on the Law of Nations, consider the politics of the dark and gloomy period preceding the Reformation which Wheaton declares "called loudly for a great teacher and reformer to arise, who should stay the ravages of this moral pestilence, and speak the unambiguous language of truth and justice to princes and people." (*Union*, p. 21) Consider that Divine Providence produced just such a man in the person of Hugo Grotius. He set the Law of Nations on a firm moral footing by founding it on the laws built into our nature by our Creator and by His will revealed to us in Scripture.

Step Five:
Original Thought

Read the excerpts from Alexander Hamilton's paper, "Americanus," in your text (pp. 17–18). This paper was written at a time when partisans of the French Revolution were urging America to become embroiled in the war that had broken out between France and England. Some Americans wanted to go to war against England. Others wanted to enter the war on England's side in order to prevent the atheistic French revolutionaries from exporting their Revolution to other European nations as they were attempting to do.

It was Hamilton's view that the United States should not "intermeddle" or intervene in the affairs of other nations. Consider his description of our *motives* and *methods* in prosecuting the War of Independence. (See p. 18) Had we gone to the aid of the French revolutionaries, we would have involved ourselves with a revolution directly opposite in character to our own — one notable for brutal terrorist acts against the French aristocracy and, at last, against any French people who opposed the Revolution. Thousands of innocent men and women were guillotined by the ruthless fanatic, Robespierre, in the last days of the Revolution. (See Hamilton's comments opposite "Designing Leaders," on p. 18) Hamilton discerned that we should not "corrupt ourselves by false comparisions" between our Revolution and that of France.

Consider also the *qualities of character* Hamilton mentions on p. 18. These qualities had united us as a people unafraid to defend our legitimate rights when invaded by others. Otherwise, we were a peace-loving people content to govern ourselves under God's laws and our own constitutional law.

After you have completed your reading of Hamilton's paper, write an essay on American foreign relations — how they are conducted today and how they could be improved in the light of the wisdom of our Founding Fathers. Try to answer these questions in your essay:

1. What are some of the dangers to our national character if we, as a nation, try to unite with other nations whose policies are anti-Christian and in opposition to our constitutional form of government?

2. What does the Bible say about being "unequally yoked with unbelievers"? Can a Christian nation make alliances with pagan nations and count on them to honor their commitments?

3. Why is it important to the other nations of the world that the United States *restore* and *maintain* its unique Christian constitutional character? Would this enable us to be an example to other nations?

4. Can we point the way to better relations between nations by respecting the independence and the natural rights of all nations and constructively defending our own nation's independence?

Step Six:

What Christian Principles and Ideas Identify the American Political Union?

Some important principles and leading ideas of American political union covered in this lesson were:

1. Daniel Webster found our *fundamental American principles* to consist of: 1) "the establishment of popular governments, on the basis of representation"; 2) the will of the majority expressed through their representatives as having the force of law; 3) subject to the fundamental law as "the supreme government of all"; and 4) the necessity of written constitutions "founded on the immediate authority of the people themselves, and regulating and restraining all the powers conferred upon government, whether legislative, executive or judicial." (*Union*, pp. 7–8)

2. The Declaration of Independence laid it down as a fundamental principle "that all men are created equal, that they are endowed by their Creator with certain inalienable rights, That among these are life, liberty, and the pursuit of happiness, That to secure these rights, governments are instituted among men, deriving their just powers from the consent of the governed...." (*Union*, p. 25)

3. George Washington believed that "the unity of government which constitutes you one people" should be justly dear to Americans. "The name American, which belongs to you in your national capacity, must always exalt the just pride of patriotism more than any appellation derived from local discriminations. With slight shades of difference, you have the same religion, manners, habits, and political principles...." (*Union*, p. 27)

4. Washington believed that "The foundation of our national policy will be laid in the pure and immutable principles of private morality, and the pre-eminence of free government be exemplified by all the attributes which can win the affections of its citizens and command the respect of the world." (*Union*, p. 14)

5. In developing a foreign policy, our Founding Fathers studied the works of the great 17th century Dutch jurist, Hugo Grotius, as well as other Protestant writers on the Law of Nations, which these writers found to be grounded in the law of God written into our natures by God and confirmed and amplified in Holy Scripture. It was a law based on justice and love, substituting for the old pagan idea of hating one's neighbor, the Christian idea of loving one's neighbor and treating him justly. (*Union*, p. 22)

6. George Washington saw that "the great rule of conduct for us in regard to foreign nations is, in extending our commercial relations to have with them as little POLITICAL connection as possible." (p. 29) He believed that we should not try to interweave our destiny with that of other nations, thus entangling our peace and prosperity, but that "taking care always to keep ourselves by suitable establishments on a respectable defensive posture, we may safely trust to temporary alliances for extraordinary emergencies." (*Union*, p. 30)

7. The Monroe Doctrine asserted "as a principle" that "the American continents... are henceforth not to be considered as subjects for future colonization by any European powers..." lest our peace and safety be threatened. James Monroe wrote: "We must support our rights or lose our character, and with it, perhaps, our liberties. A people who fail to do it can scarcely be said to hold a place among independent nations." (*Union*, p. 33)

LESSON THREE

FREE MEN,
STATES,
AND CHURCHES

By this shall all men know that ye are my disciples,
if you have love one to another.
(John 13:35)

This lesson deals with the voluntary principle in the development of both church and civil government throughout the colonies. The Congregationalists of New England, the Presbyterians and Quakers of the Middle Colonies and the Presbyterians and Baptists in the South all desired to be free and did not want to be under the rule of the Anglican Church. These sentiments gave rise to the eventual separation of the Church from the State in America — *a separation designed to protect the individual's liberty of conscience* and his right to *unite voluntarily* with the Christian denomination of his choice.

As colonial Americans studied their Bibles, it became more and more evident that the New Testament Church was the perfect illustration of the principle of voluntary union. As historian Leonard Bacon wrote of the early church:

"Churches were constituted by the spontaneous association of believers. Individuals and families, drawn toward each other by their common trust in Jesus the Christ, and their common interest in the good news concerning the kingdom of God, became a community united, not by external bonds, but by the vital force of distinctive ideas and principles. . . . Their new ideas and new sympathies and hopes were a bond of union. . . ." (*Christian History,* Vol. I, p. 16)

Because the early Christian Churches were voluntary bodies of individuals who shared a common faith in Jesus Christ as Saviour and Lord, they were able to *set a standard of union* for other Christians to follow. These early Christians demonstrated that love for one another was the *vital ingredient* needed in order to achieve unity in the church.

In America, the Pilgrims of New England gave us an example of a loving voluntary union among Christians, first in their Church and then in the "civil body politick" they established through the Mayflower Compact. The Mayflower Compact was a *civil covenant* whose wording was similar to that of their church covenant.

The Congregationalists and Presbyterians who followed the Pilgrims believed that civil as well as ecclesiastical government ought to be based on the Law of God as revealed through the Scriptures and God's Law of Nature written in our hearts. (Romans 2:14–15) William Blackstone, whose *Commentaries* on the law were closely studied by colonial Americans, wrote: "Upon these two foundations, the law of nature and the law of revelation, depend all human laws; that is to say, no human laws should be suffered to contradict these." Our forefathers also believed firmly that civil government should not be imposed on men but should be by consent of the governed. It should be a covenant between men into which they entered voluntarily.

13

STEP ONE:
PRINCIPLES TO PONDER

Thus, there are three fundamental principles developed in this lesson:

1. UNION BY THE CONSENT OF THE GOVERNED IN BOTH CHURCH AND STATE

"A Church then I take to be a voluntary Society of Men, joining themselves together of their own accord, in order to the publick worshipping of God, in such a manner as they judge acceptable to him, and effectual to the Salvation of their Souls...." (John Locke, "A Letter Concerning Toleration," *Union*, pp. 47–48)

"A civil state is a compound moral person, whose will (united by those covenants before passed) is the will of all, to the end it may use and apply the strength and riches of private persons towards maintaining the common peace, security, and well-being of all...." (Rev. John Wise, "A Vindication of New England Churches," *Union*, p. 55)

2. SEPARATION OF THE POWERS OF CHURCH AND STATE

"The Commonwealth seems to me to be a Society of Men constituted only for the procuring, preserving, and advancing their own Civil Interests." (John Locke, "A Letter Concerning Toleration," *Union*, p. 46)

"The Church and the State are distinct communities, the governments having jurisdiction partly concurrent and partly complementary: concurrent in so far as they extend over the same territory and relate to the same persons, complementary in respect to their administration of law." (William Jones Seabury, D.D., *Union*, p. 64)

3. GOD'S REVEALED AND NATURAL LAWS: THE BASIS FOR ALL HUMAN LAWS IN CHURCH AND STATE

"Thus the Law of Nature stands as an Eternal Rule to all Men, LEGISLATORS as well as others. The RULES they make for other Men's Actions, must, as well as their own ... be conformable to the Law of Nature, *i.e.*, to the Will of God." (John Locke, "Of Civil-Government, Book II" (Second Treatise), *Union*, p. 57)

"Our all-gracious Creator, Preserver, and Ruler has been pleased to discover and enforce his laws, by a revelation given to us immediately and directly from himself. This revelation is contained in the Holy Scriptures. The moral precepts delivered in the sacred oracles form a part of the law of nature, are of the same origin, and of the same obligation operating universally and perpetually...." (James Wilson, *Union*, p. 58)

"The doctrines thus delivered we call revealed or Divine law, and they are to be found only in the holy Scriptures. These precepts when revealed, are found upon comparison to be really a part of the original law of nature." (William Blackstone, *Union*, p. 64)

Step Two:
Reading for Leading Ideas

Your Reading Assignment for Step Two is: 1) "A Letter Concerning Toleration," by John Locke (*Union*, pp. 45–50); 2) "A Vindication of the Government of New England Churches," by Rev. John Wise (pp. 51–55); 3) Virginia's "Act for Establishing Religious Freedom," (pp. 59–60)

The following background material may help to place these readings in their proper historical perspective:

FEARS OF AN ANGLICAN EPISCOPACY

The letter by John Adams to the Rev. Jedediah Morse, on pp. 41–44 of your text, shows the acute concern the colonists had prior to the War of Independence that the English Parliament might impose the Anglican Church on all the colonies as the official state church.

"In Virginia," Adams notes, "the Church of England was established by law, in exclusion and without toleration of any other denomination." (p. 42) This resulted in much persecution of religious dissenters (mainly Presbyterians and Baptists). But the dissenting denominations continued to grow despite the attempts of the Anglican Church to suppress them.

TOLERATION VERSUS RELIGIOUS FREEDOM

Rev. Samuel Davies, the Great Presbyterian preacher, so much admired by his neighbor, Patrick Henry, went to England to defend the rights of the dissenting churches under the English Toleration Act. (See *T & L*, pp. 47–48 for an account of Samuel Davies' trip to England and his able defense of the religious rights of dissenters in Virginia.) The Toleration Act had been passed by Parliament in 1689. Despite Rev. Davies' efforts to secure at least toleration of dissenters in Virginia, the established church continued to persecute dissenters in many parts of the colony. This made the people very uneasy in other colonies where the Anglican Church was not the official church. What if a bishop was created for the Anglican Church in America and it was to become the established church in all the colonies?

THE POWER OF PARLIAMENT OVER THE COLONIES: LEGITIMATE OR ILLEGITIMATE?

Adams remarks: "Where is the man to be found, at this day [of religious freedom] who will believe, that the apprehension of episcopacy contributed, fifty years ago, as much as any other cause, to arouse the attention, not only of the inquiring mind, but of the common people, and urge them to close thinking on the constitutional authority of Parliament over the colonies?" (p. 41)

Since the days of England's "Glorious Revolution" of 1689, which put William and Mary on the throne as constitutional sovereigns, the power of Parliament had steadily increased. The colonists knew that if an episcopate were to be established, it would be by parliamentary edict.

As Adams explained: "The objection was not merely to the office of a Bishop, though even that was dreaded, as to the authority of Parliament, on which it must be founded.... All sensible men knew that this system could not be effected, but by Act of Parliament, and if Parliament could do this they could do all things; and what security could Americans have for life, liberty, property, or religion?"

It was no wonder that "all denominations in America... began to think of the secret, latent principle, upon which all encroachments upon us must be founded, the power of Parliament."

The colonists finally concluded that, since they were not represented in Parliament, that body had no authority over them whatsoever. But if Parliament did not rightfully possess authority over the churches in America, did the colonial legislatures possess this power? If not, what should be the relation between the Church and the State?

Some colonies — and later some states — had church establishments, others did not. (It was not until 1833 that the last church establishment in the United States, that of Massachusetts, was finally abolished.)

Whatever differences of opinion existed in the colonies as to religious liberty, John Locke's *Letter Concerning Toleration,* first published in England in 1689, had a sympathetic reading in the American colonies. Locke would have preferred full religious liberty in his own country but was willing to settle for toleration. In the *Letter Concerning Toleration,* he discusses the distinctively different roles of Church and State and concludes that their powers should be kept separate, because the one deals with men's souls and the other with their "civil interests."

Locke's *Of Civil-Government,* Second Treatise, also was widely read, quoted and paraphrased in the colonies — by clergy and laymen alike. Particularly important to the colonists in their debate with the English Parliament was Locke's writing on the Law of Nature in the Second Treatise. In the course of that ten-year debate (1765–1775) they not only contended for their rights under the British Constitution but also under God's laws which they believed, with Locke, should underlie all human law.

A VINDICATION OF THE GOVERNMENT OF NEW ENGLAND CHURCHES

In 1688, Great Britain attempted to centralize the government of the New England colonies with that of New York and New Jersey in "the New England Dominion" under the arbitrary rule of Gov. Edmund Andros. Rev. John Wise of Ipswich, Massachusetts, defied the arbitrary taxes which the governor levied without consent of the people's representatives. He was accordingly fined and imprisoned for a time.

This experience must have caused Rev. Wise to think even more deeply about the nature of righteous government in both church and state. In response to a move within the Congregational Church in 1714 to create regional ministerial associations of the Massachusetts clergy, which would have large powers over local congregations, he wrote his *Vindication of the Government of New England Churches.*

It was an eloquent plea for democratic, local self-government and voluntary union in the churches based upon God's Law of Nature as well as his Revealed Law in Scripture. Rev. Wise's paper was as applicable to civil as to ecclesiastical government. In 1772 it was reprinted and was widely read during the critical period preceding the outbreak of hostilities between the colonies and the Mother Country. (For more information on Rev. John Wise, see *Consider and Ponder,* pp. 99–103)

AN ACT FOR ESTABLISHING RELIGIOUS FREEDOM IN VIRGINIA

Full religious liberty was not achieved in Virginia until the *Act for Establishing Religious Freedom* was passed by the Virginia Legislature in 1786, a year before the Constitutional Convention. The Virginia Legislature had long been bombarded with petitions from Baptists and Presbyterians protesting being obliged to support the Anglican Church through their taxes and suffering discrimination because of their religious beliefs.

In 1784, Patrick Henry introduced legislation which he thought would correct this problem. His "general assessment" plan provided that all citizens would be taxed to support all Christian ministers of the various denominations. In describing the Act to Thomas Jefferson, James Madison wrote: "Each person when he pays his tax is to name the society to which he dedicates it, and in case of refusal to do so, the tax is to be applied to the maintenance of a school in the country." (Quoted in *James Madison— A Biography in His Own Words,* Vol. 1, p. 90. The following Madison quotations are also from Vol. 1, on pages 93 and 92 respectively.)

James Madison was very concerned about this Act, but not because he opposed the Christian religion. In a *Memorial and Remonstrance,* which he drew up in response to the Bill in 1785 and circulated throughout Virginia as a petition, he wrote:

"Whilst we assert for our selves a freedom to embrace, to profess and to observe the Religion which we believe to be of divine origin, we cannot deny an equal freedom to those whose minds have not yet yielded to the evidence which has convinced us. If this freedom be abused, it is an offence against God, not against man: To God, therefore, not to man, must an account of it be rendered. . . ."

In other words, the unbeliever was not to be forced to support the Christian Church. As for believers in Jesus Christ who were adherents of the various church denominations in Virginia, Madison asked them:

"Who does not see that the same authority which can establish Christianity, in exclusion of all other Religions, may establish with the same ease any particular sect of Christians, in exclusion of all other Sects? That the same authority which can force a citizen to contribute three pence only of his property for the support of any one establishment, may force him to conform to any other establishment in all cases whatsoever?" Furthermore, who is to decide what is a Christian church? Who will define it? He explains that "the Bill implies either that the Civil Magistrate is a competent Judge of Religious Truth; or that he may employ Religion as an engine of Civil policy." Madison believed this to be an untenable role for the civil magistrate whose powers, in his opinion, should only extend to the civil affairs of the people.

With Madison's aid, Thomas Jefferson's Bill for Establishing Religious Freedom was passed by the Virginia Legislature and became law in 1786.

Step Three:
Questions for Invention

1. John Locke wrote that toleration of those with differing religious views "is so agreeable to the Gospel of Jesus Christ," it seemed to him monstrous that men did not perceive its necessity. But such was the case in 17th and 18th century Europe. Even in Holland, which had a high degree of toleration, there was still a state church, and Independent English congregations (such as that of the Pilgrims) were only permitted to worship privately.

What then is the meaning of the word *toleration?* How does it differ from *religous liberty?* Look up the meaning of *toleration* and *religious liberty* (under *Liberty*) in Noah Webster's 1828 *American Dictionary of the English Language.*

2. Why did Locke carefully divide the powers of church and state, giving civil magistrates power only over men's "civil interests"? Did his separation of church and state imply hostility toward the Church? (Consider his remarks on page 47 of your text.)

3. According to Locke, the Church's role is "the Care of Souls" (that which pertains to the internal) while the duty of the civil magistrate is to secure the person and property of citizens (the external) and the magistrate is armed with force to punish "those that violate any other Man's Rights." In the case of conflict between the internal dictates of one's conscience and the civil laws of a land, which did Locke believe should come first and why? (See *Union,* p. 49)

4. Why did Locke not believe in extending toleration to atheists? (See *Union,* p. 49)

5. Before the Episcopal Church was disestablished in Virginia, there was a long period when Dissenters were forced to be married under its auspices, as marriages performed by their own Presbyterian or Baptist clergy were not legal. Virginia's *Act for Establishing Religious Freedom* put the Episcopal Church on an equal footing with all other denominations in Virginia. Financial support of churches was voluntary, not compelled by law. Prior to passage of the Act, however, some men, like Patrick Henry and George Washington, thought it not unreasonable to tax the people for the support of the denomination of their choice. What do you think was wrong with this idea? What principle did it violate? (See *Union,* p. 59)

6. Why do you think God might want men to

enter into covenant with Him to form their civil governments?

7. What does the Golden Rule for man's conduct (see Matt. 7:12) have to do with the Law of Nature? (See also Rev. Wise's comments on how each man may discover the Law of Nature that is to govern his own conduct, p. 52, last paragraph.)

8. What is the "property in nature" most men naturally possess which is essential "for cementing of parts" into a union and without which government "would soon moulder and dissolve?" (See Rev. Wise, p. 53)

9. Rev. Wise believed that God had stamped a love of liberty in men's nature. But is this liberty a license to do whatever one wants — to do "one's own thing" no matter what the consequences? (See Rev. Wise, p. 54 and Locke in "Of Civil-Government" quoted on p. 72)

10. How does Rev. Wise define "a civil state"? (See p. 55. See also Rev. Seabury's definition on p. 62) How does this definition differ from modern, secular concepts of a civil state?

STEP FOUR:

FURTHER STUDY OF PRINCIPLES AND LEADING IDEAS

The object of Step Four in this lesson is to understand more deeply the Law of Nature which is so greatly misunderstood today and often associated with godless rationalism. In order to understand it as the founding Fathers did — which was in relation to God's Revealed Law in Scripture — read the extracts from John Locke's *The Reasonableness of Christianity* on pp. 72–90 of your text.

Locke wrote this treatise in order to convince the Deists of the necessity and truth of Biblical revelation which they had rejected as unnecessary.

"But if there be not a great Number of Deists, and that the preventing their Increase be not worth every true Christian's Care and Endeavours, those who have been so loud against them have been much to blame.... For these therefore, I take the Liberty to say ... that I chiefly designed my Book; ..." (John Locke, "A Second Vindication of the Reasonableness of Christianity," *The Works of John Locke Esq.*, John Churchill, London (1714), Vol. II, par. XIX, p. 595)

THE MORAL LAW OF MOSES

In this work Locke discusses the difference between the Ceremonial Laws of the Jews and the Moral Law of Moses: "Thus then as to the Law in short. The Civil and Ritual part of the Law delivered by Moses obliges not Christians, though to the Jews it were a part of the Law of Works; it being a part of the Law of Nature, that Man ought to obey every positive Law of God.... But the Moral part of Moses's Law, or the Moral Law (which is every where the same, the eternal Rule of Right) obliges Christians and all Men every where, and is to all Men the standing Law of Works." (See *Union*, p. 75)

THE LIMITED ROLE OF REASON

Locke points out that despite the efforts of pagan philosophers to understand God, it was in a "state of Darkness and Error, in reference to the True God [that] our Saviour found the World. But the clear Revelation he brought with him, dissipated this Darkness...." (p. 84)

Note particularly what Locke has to say about the inability of *unassisted* reason to arrive at a complete understanding of the Law of Nature. (See pp. 86–90) For example: "Next to the knowledge of one God; maker of all Things; a clear 'knowledge of their Duty' was wanting to Mankind.

"It would seem by the little that has hitherto been done in it, that 'tis too hard a Task for unassisted Reason, to establish Morality in all its Parts upon its true Foundations, with a clear and convincing Light. ... We see how unsuccessful in this the Attempts of Philosophers were before our Saviour's time...." (p. 86)

THE PENALTIES FOR TRANSGRESSING THE LAW OF NATURE

In his Second Treatise ("Of Civil-Government," Book II), John Locke asserted that "the State of Nature has a Law of Nature to govern it, which obliges everyone: and Reason, which is that Law, teaches all Mankind, who will but consult it, that being all equal and independent, no one ought to harm another in his Life, Health, Liberty, or Possessions." (*Christian History*, Vol. 1, John Locke, "Of Civil-Government, Book II," p. 58:6) But he recognized that sinful man too often was prone to ignore the God-given gift of reason or to pervert it to do evil.

"In transgressing the Law of Nature, the Offender declares himself to live by another Rule, than that of common Reason and Equity, which is that measure God has set to the actions of Men, for their Mutual Security; and so he becomes dangerous to Mankind, the Tye, which is to secure them from Injury and Violence, being slighted and broken by him." (*Ibid.*, p. 59:8)

By violating the law, such a man departs from "the right Rule of Reason... and declares himself to quit the Principles of human Nature, and to be a noxious Creature...." (*Ibid.*, p. 59:10)

Where there is no civil government among men, a State of Nature exists and "every Man... has a Power to kill a Murderer, both to deter others from doing the like Injury, which no Reparation can compensate... and also to secure Men from the attempts of a Criminal, who having renounced Reason, the common Rule and Measure, God hath given to Mankind, hath by the unjust Violence and Slaughter he hath committed upon one, declared War against all Mankind.... And upon this is grounded that great Law of Nature, *whoso sheddeth Man's Blood, by Man shall his Blood be shed*. And *Cain* was so fully convinced, that every one had a Right to destroy such a Criminal, that after the Murther of his Brother, he cries out, *Every one that findeth me, shall slay me; so plain was it writ in the Hearts of all Mankind.*" (*Ibid.*, p. 60:11)

But because "passion and revenge" will carry men too far when they are judges of those who have injured them personally, John Locke said that "Confusion and Disorder" would follow, and "therefore God hath certainly appointed Government to restrain the partiality and violence of Men living in a State of Nature." (*Ibid.*, p. 60:12)

GOD'S TWO WAYS OF COMMUNICATING HIS WILL

Some writers have accused the New England clergy of the colonial and revolutionary eras of succumbing to the doctrines of "rationalism" because of their frequent references to reason and the Law of Nature. It is important to recognize, however, that as Alice M. Baldwin explained in her landmark study, *The New England Clergy and the American Revolution,* "The clergy... of the 18th century as those of the 17th believed Reason and Nature but the voice of God and the laws of Nature as truly those of God as the laws found in the Scripture. This they said repeatedly and thus gave a sacred significance to the laws of nature and the arguments from Reason.... There was no conflict in their minds between the divine and natural law. They were the same [*i.e.*, both were of God]." (See Baldwin, pp. 28–29)

Write a brief essay on the Law of Nature as understood by John Locke and our Founding Fathers.

STEP FIVE: ORIGINAL THOUGHT

As we have learned, our Founding Fathers believed in the necessity of "a frequent recurrence to fundamental principles" in order to preserve their liberty. We have also seen that some of these "fundamental principles" were capsulized in the Declaration of Independence which provided the foundation on which the Framers of the Constitution later built the framework for our national government. To the Framers, the United States Constitution rested on "the transcendent law of nature and nature's God, which declares that the safety and happiness of society are the objects at which all political institutions aim...." (James Madison, *The Federalist Papers*, No. 43)

Turn to the excerpts from the *Declaration of Independence* in your text, pp. 25–26, and note the statement of rights set forth beginning with: "We hold these Truths to be self-evident...."

AMERICA'S FOUNDING COVENANT

As you have learned, *government by consent of the governed* was one of the Founding Fathers' "fundamental principles." They believed, as had the Pilgrim Fathers, that men had a God-given right to come together voluntarily to form their "civil body politick," by solemn covenant or compact. The Declaration of Independence, as a covenant document, ends with an affirmation of firm reliance on the protection of Divine Providence as the Framers pledged to support the Declaration with their lives, their fortunes and their sacred honor.

The colonists had long absorbed the covenantal aspect of government from the many influential New England pastors whose sermons were circulated widely throughout the colonies prior to the War of Independence. The state constitutions that preceded the United States Constitution show the strong influence of covenantal thinking.

Daniel J. Elazar, a leading scholar researching the covenantal origins of America's unique federal system, says that the Declaration of Independence is the covenant that bound the American people together in "a shared moral vision as well as common interests." (See his analysis of the Declaration as a covenant in "The American System as a Federal Democracy" in *Teaching About Federal Democracy*, a booklet published by the Center for the Study of Federalism, Temple University, Philadelphia, Pennsylvania, p. 15)

The ''shared moral vision'' of Americans, expressed in the Declaration of Independence, was translated into practical governmental terms for the nation by the Constitution and the Bill of Rights.

WHEN SOCIOLOGICAL LAW SUPPLANTED THE HIGHER LAW

It used to be considered necessary to study the ''higher law'' background of the Constitution, in order to understand it properly, but many modern teachers of jurisprudence believe that the Law of Nature was a mere ''legal fiction'' of the 18th century and need not be considered in interpreting the Constitution today.

By the late 19th and early 20th century, decisions of the United States Supreme Court bench began to take on a sociological aspect. The renowned Oliver Wendell Holmes, Jr., held that law is only ''the expression of the dominant force in the community.'' He held that values were relative to the *mores* of a society at a given time, but that there were no timeless, absolute moral values. According to the new philosophy of *pragmatism,* whatever the people wanted began to be the new norm.

The modern idea of ''the living Constitution'' holds that it is to be interpreted through the lens of society's constantly changing standards of right and wrong — not by the immutable standards of the Higher Law, *i.e.,* God's laws revealed in Scripture and in His Law of Nature. Holmes believed that ''the proximate test of a good government is that the dominant power has its way.'' (Cited in Robert K. Dornan and Csaba Vedlik, Jr., *Judicial Supremacy: The Supreme Court on Trial,* p. 52)

Consider the following questions: 1) What has happened to our country as immutable standards have been abandoned in the lives of the people and then in constitutional interpretations of the United States Supreme Court? 2) What are some good state laws that have been struck down by the United States Supreme Court and declared unconstitutional? 3) What can we do to help restore our constitutional system to the original intent of the Framers and why is it important to do this?

Write an essay on the Higher Law in relation to the Constitution addressing yourself to these questions.

STEP SIX:

WHAT CHRISTIAN PRINCIPLES AND IDEAS IDENTIFY THE AMERICAN POLITICAL UNION?

1. The American political union was based on the Higher Law of God seen in His Law of Nature and His Revealed Law in Scripture. (See *Union,* pp. 57–58)

2. The original American principle of separation of church and state was a mutually supportive and friendly one. It was adopted by the Framers of the Constitution in order to protect the religious liberty of all citizens from coercion by civil government into belonging to a particular religious denomination and in order to protect the right of citizens to unite voluntarily with other Christians in the church body of their choice. (See Dr. Seabury's comments on the alternatives to the Founding Father view of church and state on pp. 64–66)

3. The voluntary principle in the formation of both church and state was acknowledged by the Founding Fathers as essential. Men had a right to form churches voluntarily and also to come together in solemn covenant to form their civil governments. (See Rev. John Wise's words in your text, at the top of p. 55 and John Locke's on p. 34)

THE DEVELOPMENT OF CHRISTIAN UNION

For as we have many members in one body, and all members have not the same office;
so we, being many, are one body in Christ, and everyone members one of another.
(Romans 12:4–5)

This lesson surveys the development of local self-government in the early Church as it confronted that great centralized despotism, the Roman Empire, with a new kind of union, one in which diversity was not swallowed up by union. The ecclesiastical historian, Johann Lorenz von Mosheim (1694–1755), explains:

"The churches, in those times, were entirely independent; none of them subject to any foreign jurisdiction, but each one governed by its own rulers and its own laws. For, though the churches founded by the apostles, had this particular deference shewn them, that they were consulted in difficult and doubtful cases; yet they had no juridical authority, nor sort of supremacy over the others, nor the least right to enact laws for them. Nothing, on the contrary, is more evident than the perfect equality that reigned among the primitive churches...." (*Union*, p. 120)

From their own study of the history of the New Testament churches, our Pilgrim and Puritan ancestors learned much concerning the Christian way to unite. In this lesson you will study the first attempt at colonial union in America, the New England Confederacy (1643), which united four New England colonies whose people "came into these parts of America with one and ye same end and aime... to advance the kingdom of our Lord Jesus Christ, to

injoye ye liberties of ye Gospell in puritie with peace...." (*Union*, p. 309)

STEP ONE:
PRINCIPLES TO PONDER

1. THE PRINCIPLE OF CHRISTIAN LIBERTY DISPLACES ANCIENT CENTRALIZATION

"The ancient centralization lay prostrate. It had fallen before the principle which it had for ages overpowered.... It was the liberty to live according to the law of love proclaimed by Christ the Lord. No liberty of antiquity could compare with it. No dominion of antiquity could repress it." (Samuel Eliot, "History of Liberty," *Union*, pp. 212–214)

2. THE EARLY CHRISTIAN CHURCHES EMBRACED THE DEMOCRATIC PRINCIPLE

"In those early times, every Christian church consisted of the people, their leaders, and the ministers, or deacons.... The people were, undoubtedly, the first in authority; for the apostles shewed, by their own example, that nothing of moment was to be carried on or determined without the consent of the assembly...." (John Lawrence Mosheim,

"An Ecclesiastical History," *Union*, pp. 116–117)

3. THE REPRESENTATIVE PRINCIPLE WAS ADOPTED BY THE EARLY CHRISTIAN CHURCHES

"It was . . . the assembly of the people, which chose their own rulers and teachers, or received them by free and authoritive consent, when recommended by others." (Mosheim, *Union*, p. 117)

4. THE UNIVERSAL CHURCH BECOMES ONE VAST REPUBLIC

"During a great part of [the second] century, the Christian churches were independent of each other; nor were they joined together by association, confederacy, or any other bonds but those of charity. Each Christian assembly was a little state, governed by its own laws. . . . But in process of time, all the Christian churches of a province were formed into one large ecclesiastical body, which, like confederate states, assembled at certain times, in order to deliberate about the common interests of the whole. . . . and the universal church had now the appearance of one vast republic, formed by a combination of a great number of little states." (John Lawrence Mosheim, *Union*, pp. 127–128)

5. THE FIRST CONCEPTION OF AMERICAN UNION WAS INSPIRED BY THE THEOCRATIC PRINCIPLE

"The first conception of an American Union entertained by the founders of New England was to join in political bonds only those colonies in which the people were of a similar way of thinking in theology, when, in the spirit of a theocracy they aimed to form a Christian State in the bosom of the Church. This was embodied in the New England Confederacy (1643 to 1684)." (Richard Frothingham, "The Rise of the Republic of the United States," *Union*, p. 304)

6. THE NEW-ENGLAND CONFEDERACY COMBINED THE PRINCIPLES OF LOCAL SELF-GOVERNMENT AND UNION

"The two elements of local government and union were first combined in a common polity in the New-England Confederacy. . . .

"The four colonies in this compact, as belonging to 'one nation,' formed a league for self-defence and the common welfare. . . . It was specified, that the vital subject of taxation should be left to the several local jurisdictions, and that the commissioners should not intermeddle with their administrative

functions; thereby recognizing the inviolability of local government. The Union element, represented in the Board of Commissioners, was but feebly provided for; the board being little more than a consulting body. . . ." (Richard Frothingham, *Union*, pp. 307, 312)

7. NECESSARY TO COLONIAL UNION WAS A WIDESPREAD CONVICTION "AS TO FUNDAMENTAL PRINCIPLES"

"The combination of local self-government and of union [in the New-England Confederacy] was made before the colonists had attained to just conceptions of what should be the basis of such a union. . . . The fraternal spirit between them as communities was feeble. . . . Conviction as to fundamental principles is a necessary condition to a superstructure of law; and this had not been reached." (Richard Frothingham, *Union*, p. 313)

STEP TWO:
READING FOR LEADING IDEAS

A thoughtful reading of the writings of the Founding Fathers and of early histories of the founding period reveals how closely related *union* and *liberty* were in the minds of the colonists.

Consider this passage from Richard Frothingham's *Rise of the Republic* dealing with the period when Great Britain blockaded the Port of Boston in retaliation for the protests of Massachusetts against taxation without representation:

"On the flag floating over popular gatherings was the motto UNION & LIBERTY. . . . it seemed as though that generation realized that there could be no union without liberty, and no genuine liberty without the power there was in union to protect it." (*Union*, p. 572)

FROM THE PILGRIMS TO THE PATRIOTS

Our forefathers, from the Pilgrims of the 17th Century to the Patriots of the 18th and early 19th centuries, grounded their views of liberty and union in God's laws as revealed in the Holy Scriptures or in His Law of Nature. Recollect that to them the Law of Nature was God's law written in our hearts (Romans 2:14–15) and confirmed and amplified in Holy Scripture. They agreed with William Blackstone that "Upon these two foundations, the law of nature and the law of revelation, depend all human laws; that is to say, no human laws should be suffered to contradict these." (*Christian History*, Vol. 1, p. 143)

Well into the 19th century Americans continued to perceive the Scriptural basis of these important concepts. As you will learn in your Reading Assignment, New England historian Samuel Eliot wrote of how the union of the early Christians confronted "ancient centralization" and prepared the way for its eventual displacement by the Christian idea of man and government which honors the individual as God's creation and thus respects individual liberty, self-government and union under the laws of God.

Your Reading Assignment will also take you into extended extracts from Mosheim's *An Ecclesiastical History*. Mosheim was a German theologian and historian who traced the history of Christianity from its beginnings. He discerned that the first Christian churches were little self-governing, representative bodies.

Note, too, that the laws decreed by the "synods" or "councils" *began to curtail the rights of the individual congregations*. These councils were useful, however, in one important respect: They were a model, though an imperfect one, of "one vast republic, formed by a combination of a great number of little states." (See your text, p. 128)

Read Samuel Eliot's overview of the history of liberty and union in your text, pp. 212–214. Then read the following extracts from Mosheim: "The Governments of the Churches," pp. 115–120; "The Rise of Church Councils," pp. 127–128; and "Religious Monarchy Established by Imperceptible Steps," pp. 130–131.

STEP THREE:
QUESTIONS FOR INVENTION

1. Why do you suppose Americans, like 19th century historian Samuel Eliot, viewed centralized government as pagan, unchristian government? Why do Americans today tend to view centralized government as either a blessing or a necessary evil?

2. What did Eliot believe Christians have to demonstrate before Christian union can be placed on a firm foundation? Why is this true? (See Eliot, p. 214)

3. Why did Mosheim believe that the form of government of the first Christian church at Jerusalem "must be esteemed as of divine institution?" (See *Union*, p. 116)

4. In the early Christian churches, who were

the first in authority? (See *Union*, p. 116)

5. What were the offices of the early Christian Church and how were they filled? (See *Union*, p. 117–118)

6. Is there an analogy between the office of the bishops in the early church, who were servants, not masters, of their congregations, and the term "public servant" used in America to describe our elected public officials? How can we hold our public officials to that same standard today?

7. How did the early bishops make decisions or enact laws without the consent of the presbyters and the people? (See *Union*, p. 120)

8. What were the only bonds of union of the churches during the early part of the second century? (See *Union*, p. 128)

9. Mosheim describes the development of the church from completely independent bodies to "the appearance of one vast republic, formed by a combination of a great number of little states." What caused the churches to cease being a federation of locally self-governing bodies? (See your text, pp. 127–128)

10. In many modern nations, the proponents of socialism have taken over governments by sudden revolutions. This has not happened in America. What is the method that the proponents of socialism have used here to change the form of our United States government? How is it similar to what happened in the early Christian church? Do you think that a *return* to the constitutional system of government conceived by our Founding Fathers is likely to come about rapidly or gradually and what is needed to effect this change?

STEP FOUR:
FURTHER STUDY OF PRINCIPLES AND LEADING IDEAS

If you wish to study the development of the early Christian Church in greater depth and detail, read the selections from Mosheim's *Ecclesiastical History*, *Union*, pp. 93–114, 121–127 and 132–138.

PAGAN RELIGIONS — 1 A.D.

Note that when Jesus was born into the world, there were many strange religions and philosophies that dominated men's minds. (Text, pp. 93–100) Also note these words of Jacob Von Falke on p. 99:

"The Roman had an immense toleration for alien gods . . . when he conquered a foreign state, and destroyed a foreign city, he made no scruple of transporting the patron gods bodily to Rome. . . ." But, as another author points out: "There was a law in Rome, that no God should be worshipped without the consent of the senate . . . and by virtue of this law, the first Christians were exposed to all manner of cruelties." (Algernon Sidney, "Discourses on Government," *Union,* p. 100; Sidney's writings were widely read in colonial America.)

In his discussion of pagan religions in the first century, Mosheim styles *gnosticism* as the most detrimental to Christianity, as its adherents tried to blend its notions, which were foreign to Christianity, into the Christian faith. (See text, pp. 113 and 125)

PAGAN PHILOSOPHY — 1 A.D.

Among the philosophies that Mosheim styles as "the most vicious" were those of the Epicureans and Academics which "struck at the foundations of all religion." (See text, p. 97)

There were also other pagan philosophers, such as Plato and Aristotle, who were very popular among educated Romans and who speculated as to the existence of one God, deducing the existence of a Creator from the creation. Neither Greek nor Roman philosophy, however, contained a body of law such as the Jews possessed, *i.e.,* a law that claimed divine sanction and authority.

Thus, when Aristotle discussed the different forms of government known to men and their differing laws, he was perplexed:

"But what are good laws has not yet been clearly explained; the old difficulty remains. The goodness or badness, justice or injustice of laws depends of necessity on the constitutions of states." (Aristotle's *Politics,* Book III, Chapter 11.)

Laws might be adjudged good or bad according to the form of government of a state, whether the government be by one man, a few, or the many. Laws considered good under one system might be considered bad under another. Thus law appeared to be relative.

THE JEWS — 1 A.D.
THE DEPOSITARY OF THE LAW

Consider the state of religion in the Jewish na-tion at A.D. 1 with its divisions into three sects. (See text, pp. 101–103.) The Jews had the Law of God in the Ten Commandments and the Book of the Law, but it was very differently interpreted by the three theological schools of thought of the Pharisees, the Sadducees and the Essenes. (See p. 102)

In addition to the extracts from Mosheim's *Ecclesiastical History* given in the text, there are other passages in his book which give further details on the views of the Law held by the three sects:

- The Pharisees added to the written law of God an oral or unwritten law handed down by tradition.

- Both the Sadducees and the Essenes rejected the traditional, unwritten law of the Pharisees and relied wholly on the written Word of God.

These three sects also held differing views concerning the written law of God:

- The Pharisees believed the Scriptures had two meanings: the literal and the figurative.

- The Sadducees held only to the literal meaning.

- The Essenes largely disagreed with both, maintaining that the words of the Law were of no authority, only the things expressed by them which are images indicative of sacred and divine things.

THE ADVENT OF JESUS CHRIST

In this state of contending beliefs among the pagan philosophers and heathen religions and even among the Jews who were "the sole depositary of the . . . knowledge of one Supreme God" (text, p. 103), there was great need of the Saviour. See pp. 104–107 for Mosheim's summary of the earthly life of Jesus Christ.

Mosheim relates how Jesus converted "a great number of Jews" and how, on His resurrection from the grave, He gave to His disciples the Divine Commission to preach salvation to all men. By His gift of the Holy Spirit, He enabled His Apostles to preach with persuasive eloquence. He appointed Paul, who was wise in both Jewish and Grecian learning, to be His apostle to the Gentiles.

THE CHURCH AFTER THE AGE OF THE APOSTLES

By the second century, many learned Christian minds became imbued with the ideas of the pagan philosophers. See John Locke's comment on the influence of pagan philosophy on Christian writers after the age of the apostles in your text, on p. 124. See also Mosheim, p. 129 on "Chimerical Philosophy Attempts to Overturn the Teaching of Jesus Christ."

In the second century, Mosheim also relates that "many unnecessary rites and ceremonies" were added to the Church which contributed to destroy "the beautiful simplicity of the gospel" and focused people's minds more and more on *external religion* rather than on the *internal conversion of the heart* so necessary to genuine Christianity.

THE CHRISTIAN CHURCH IN THE THIRD CENTURY

In the third century, as you have already learned in Step Two, the church moved more and more toward a monarchical system of government. Mosheim believed that this change in the form of ecclesiastical government was followed by a corrupted clergy.

"Many bishops now affected the state of princes, and especially those who had charge of the more populous and wealthy congregations; for they sat on thrones, surrounded by their ministers... and dazzled the eyes and the minds of the populace with their splendid attire." (*Mosheim's Ecclesiastical History*, Vol. I, Robert Carter & Brothers, New York (1839), p. 165)

THE CHURCH UNDER CONSTANTINE

Note that, in discussing the gradual changes in the structure of the Church after its adoption by the Roman emperor, Constantine, Mosheim says that Constantine did not institute the episcopal form of government over the churches; he found it already existing. He made no alterations in the government of the church EXCEPT that "he assumed to himself the supreme power over this sacred body, and the right of modelling and governing it in such a manner, as should be most conducive to the public good...." (*Union*, p. 135)

In the light of what you have read, answer the following questions:

1. What is likely to happen to the civil government of a nation when the religious government of the church or churches becomes strongly external and is imposed by a hierarchy? Where do we see evidence of this in our country today?

2. When people feel free to interpret the Bible loosely, adding to it the opinions of other writers as equally authoritative, what happens to the Gospel?

3. As Americans have loosely interpreted our United States Constitution, adding to it the opinions of others whose views are foreign to the intent of the Framers, what has happened to constitutional government in America? Is there a connection between our views of the Gospel and our views of government?

4. Should the Constitution be changed by reinterpretation in the light of current *mores* or should it be changed by Amendment?

5. What general pagan philosophy of life is shared by many Americans today? How do we see it reflected in our national life?

STEP FIVE: ORIGINAL THOUGHT

Consider Samuel Eliot's words concerning the work of the early Christians: to prepare the union of the future. It was, as he said, a union that could not be achieved at once; it could only be prepared. Was this not also true in the case of our forefathers? Christian union took a long time to develop in America, but it was a steady, step-by-step development from a solid base. Note that at every step a kind of union was sought that would preserve local self-government.

The *first step* was when a sturdy band of Separatists from the Church of England, known to us as the Pilgrims, planted a colony on the inhospitable shores of New England in 1620. In reading the New Testament, they saw the gospel in all its simplicity and purity — and the simplicity and purity of the Church's government as it was in the beginning. It was but natural to them to transfer from the ecclesiastical to the civil realm the concepts of government they found in the Scriptures.

THE MAYFLOWER COMPACT — 1620

The compact they drew up in Cape Cod harbor on November 11, 1620 united both Pilgrims and "strangers" (the people traveling with them who were not of their congregation) into one civil community by solemn covenant. The Mayflower Compact proclaimed that having undertaken the planting of their colony "for ye glorie of God, and advancemente of ye Christian faith" they "solemnly & mutualy in ye presence of God, and of one another, covenant & combine our selves to-geather into a civill body politick, for our better ordering and preservation...." (*Christian History*, Vol. I, p. 204)

Theirs was the first of many such "plantation covenants" in New England which united the people into communities by covenant just as they had been united as churches by their church covenants.

THE FIRST
AMERICAN CONSTITUTION — 1638

The *second step* toward union was when three little congregations left the Massachusetts Bay colony and went into the Connecticut valley where they united as a civil community and produced "a written constitution for the government of the colony; the 'first written constitution', it has been called, 'in the history of nations.'" (See *Christian History*, Vol. I, pp. 249–256, for a fascinating account of the founding of this colony)

"That Charter of public rule was a document far in advance of anything the world had ever seen, in its recognition of the origin of all civil authority as derived under God, from the agreement and covenant of the whole body of the governed." The author here quoted, George Leon Walker, goes on to observe that "the form of civil government here established was simply an extension to the domain of secular affairs of the principles already adopted in religious matters — the mutual covenant and agreement of those associated, as under God the ultimate law."

See p. 252 of *Christian History*, Vol. I, for an account of the role of Rev. Thomas Hooker in producing the Connecticut Constitution. Here John Fiske remarks in his *Beginnings of New England*:

"The most noteworthy features of the Connecticut republic was that it was a federation of independent towns, and that all attributes of sovereignty not expressly granted to the General Court remained, as of original right, in the towns...."

THE NEW ENGLAND CONFEDERACY — 1643

The *third step* toward union was when four New England colonies — New-Plymouth, Massachusetts Bay, Connecticut, and New Haven — united to defend themselves against attack and to further their common concerns.

Read about the New England Confederacy of 1643 in *Union*, on p. 304 and pp. 307–312 and then write a short essay on this Confederacy as an important step toward eventual union of all the American colonies. Describe its *positive achievements* as well as it *one important defect* (see p. 312).

In writing your essay, consider: 1) What two fundamental aims did they have in forming this confederacy? (See Article 2, text, p. 310); 2) Did the union of the New England colonies involve interference with the local government of the member colonies? (See, Article 7, on p. 310); 3) What kind of agreements were the commissioners of the United Colonies empowered to make? (See Article 8, p. 311)

STEP SIX:

WHAT CHRISTIAN PRINCIPLES AND IDEAS IDENTIFY THE AMERICAN POLITICAL UNION?

1. The structure of the early Church greatly influenced our Pilgrim and Puritan ancestors in their approach to the structuring of their churches — and their civil governments. Their study of the Scripture taught them that the early Church was both democratic and republican. (See Mosheim, *Union*, pp. 116–117)

2. The Pilgrims found the basis for their church government in the New Testament Church. Their church government was, in turn, the model for their body politic in the New World. The Mayflower Compact (1620) is a covenantal document used to establish civil rather than ecclesiastical government.

3. The Mayflower Compact united not only those of the Pilgrims' congregation, but the "strangers" who came from other theological perspectives (*i.e.,* Anglicans, Puritans, and nominal Christians). All who signed the document agreed to live by its rules and by the laws that should hereafter be made by the community and its governmental representatives. (See text of the Mayflower Compact in *Christian History*, Vol. I, p. 204)

4. At every step of colonial union the colonists endeavored to protect local self-government. This is seen in both America's first Constitution, The Fundamental Orders of Connecticut (1638) which united three towns, and the New England Confederacy (1643) which united four colonies: Massachusetts, Plymouth, Connecticut, and New Haven. (*Union*, pp. 308–312)

LESSON FIVE

THE SEARCH FOR SANCTITY OF LAW

Thou shalt have no other Gods before me.
(Exodus 20:3)

The texts for this lesson examine the great governmental problem that faced ancient Rome, the early Christian Church, and later the Holy Roman Empire led by pope and emperor: What gives law its sanction and its power over men's hearts? Must it not be its sacred nature that caused men to want to obey it? Can men long be ruled by laws they do not believe have a sacred base? To answer these questions, we need to understand two important words: "sanctity" and "sanction" as they pertain to law.

"The two words 'sanction' and 'sanctity' proceed out of a common root idea. They both involve the notion of a compelling power over the minds of men, the latter of somewhat more spiritual or intellectual nature than the former. [The sanctity of the law] is, therefore, that quality or those qualities in the law which constrain the mind of the citizen-subject to obedience... [first] the conviction of the legitimacy of the source of the law, and, secondly, of the rationality of its content." (John W. Burgess, *The Sanctity of Law,* in *Union,* p. 146)

In his *American Dictionary of the English Language* (1828), Noah Webster defines the word "sanctity" as: "holiness; state of being sacred or holy.... Goodness; purity; godliness.... Sacredness; solemnity; as the *sanctity* of an oath." He defines the verb "to sanction" as: "To ratify; to confirm; to give validity or authority."

Bearing these definitions in mind, it becomes clear that what gives laws their *authority* (sanction) is their *sacredness* (sanctity).

- The Romans addressed themselves to the problem of the sanctity of law but failed to solve it, although they attempted to do so during the period of the Empire by elevating the Emperor to the status of a god.

- The Holy Roman Empire with the Pope at its apex gave sanctity to the law, but papal abuses gave impetus to the Reformation in which independent nation states, in their turn, had to address themselves to the same question: Who or what gives the law its sanction?

- The religious reformers of the Great Reformation looked to the immutable standards of the Bible, rather than to kings, emperors or popes, to find the sanctity of the law. They found the models for all legitimate human laws in the Ten Commandments and in the Two Commandments of their Lord and Saviour. *They found that only the sanctity of the Word gives laws their sanction and their power over the minds of men.*

The reformers stressed the individual's relation to God through faith and gave the Bible to the people in their own languages. *In giving the responsibility of interpreting the Bible to the individual,* rather than to a priestly hierarchy, the Reformation also awakened the individual's intellect.

"Science, literature, invention, social life, political reform, — all were stimulated by it," said Rev. S. J. Foljambe, in 1876, in a remarkable Election Sermon, "The Hand of God in American History." God had also prepared a place for a race of men who understood the Biblical base of the sanctity of law — a place where the new world in religion and intellect would find full scope. As Rev. Foljambe also observed: "When he had created a stalwart race, and ordained them for the settlement of this country, and for laying the foundations of a higher civilization than the world had yet seen... then he suddenly dropped the veil from this continent, and there arose before the astonished vision of the nations the splendors of the Western World." (See his sermon in *Consider and Ponder,* p. 48)

STEP ONE:
PRINCIPLES TO PONDER

1. THE LAW THAT MAINTAINS EVERY COMMONWEALTH: THE TEN COMMANDMENTS

"This rule is the LAW OF NATURE... set further in writing in the decaloge or ten commandments: and after reduced by Christ our saveour into these two wordes: Thou shalt love thy lorde God above all things, and thy neighbour as thyself.... In this lawe is comprehended all justice, the perfit way to serve and glorifie God, and the right meane to rule every man particularly, and all men generally: and the only way to mayntayne every commonwealth...." (John Ponet, "A Short Treatise of Politicke Power" (1556) in *Union,* p. 140)

2. THE RIGHT PRINCIPLES OF HUMAN CONDUCT REVEALED BY THE LAW OF REASON AND THE GOSPEL LAW

"As men we have God for our King, and are under the Law of Reason; as Christians, we have Jesus the Messiah for our King, and are under the Law reveal'd by him in the Gospel." (John Locke, "The Reasonableness of Christianity" (1695) in *Union,* p. 140)

3. THE BIBLE IS THE SOURCE OF SANCTITY OF LAW

"The sanctity of law was re-established [by John Calvin] on the basis of divinity of source, morality of content, and certainty of execution. Under his regime Geneva, from having been a most licentious, vicious, and immoral community, became the model city of the age; and its union with the other Swiss cantons was the chief force in the production of the Switzerland of modern times...." (John W. Burgess, *Union,* p. 194)

4. THE STATE EXISTS FOR THE INDIVIDUAL: AN AMERICAN PRINCIPLE THAT REFLECTS THE CHRISTIAN IDEA OF MAN

"Experience leads us to this conclusion... and so does theology. God has not created the world for the sake of the universal man, but for the sake of individual persons...." (Roger Bacon, *Union,* p. 174)

"The state is a society of moral beings. The state does not absorb individuality, but exists for the better obtaining of the true ends of each individual and of society collectively.... The state does not make right, but is founded upon it...." (Francis Lieber, "A Manual of Political Ethics" (1874), *Union,* p. 14)

STEP TWO:
READING FOR LEADING IDEAS

Before beginning your reading assignment for this lesson, consider the following historical survey of mankind's search for sanctity of law:

THE ROMAN EMPEROR AS PONTIFEX MAXIMUS

When the Roman Republic, with its complicated system of representative assemblies based on class, degenerated into the military dictatorship of Julius Caeser and his successors, *the Roman emperors sought to embody the sanctity of law in their own persons.* The Emperor was made Pontifex Maximus, or chief priest, of all the religions in the republic of which there were a great many all competing for men's minds. The only compelling religious power was the person of the emperor. On his death he was declared to be a god to whom men were obliged to bow down and worship. But as historian John W. Burgess observes, the "lack of a compelling power of a religious or moral nature over the spirits of men was bound, sooner or later, to lead to a catastrophe." (See your text, p. 151, for his comments on the Roman system.)

Christians, of course, could not worship the emperor as a God. Their refusal to do so was deemed a crime under Roman law, as were the secret meetings of their church. But, as Burgess notes, persecution of the Christians only made their case known to the people so that the cause of Christ began to gain many new adherents among the Romans. By the fourth century, persecution "had driven almost everybody into the new religious organization." (*Union,* p. 151)

A CHURCH INDIRECTLY GOVERNED BY THE STATE

When the Emperor Constantine adopted the church and gave it his protection, he could not proclaim himself its Pontifex Maximus, *because Christians continued to discriminate carefully between church and civil office.* They knew that God's will could not be transmitted to them by an emperor or other civil authority. Nevertheless, they acknowledged the Emperor as the supreme ruler of the civil state, and it was he who presided as president over the council called in 325 to settle the creed of the Church (the Council of Nicea). So, in a sense, by his protection of the church, the Emperor made himself its head.

THE STATE INDIRECTLY GOVERNED BY THE CHURCH

But under the Holy Roman Empire that arose on the ashes of the Western Roman Empire (which collapsed in 476 A.D.), it was the Pope, who became the supreme power over the state as well as the church. *It was now the pope who gave the law its sanctity.* The fundamental principle of the new system was that God ruled the world and made known His will for the government of men through the Pope, the supreme Head of the Christian Church who conferred upon the Emperor the authority to execute the commands of God in civil affairs. (See *Union,* p. 160)

THE RISE OF NATION STATES

When this Empire, in its turn, began to break up into independent nation states whose rulers *each* claimed to be transmitting the divine will, *imperial unity* under the Pope began to be undermined. Gradually the Empire was transformed into a confederation of "quasi-sovereign states," whose rulers claimed supreme civil power within their states. Nevertheless, the rulers continued to seek the pope's blessing on their civil rule in order *to give sanctity to their laws.*

THE RENAISSANCE OR REVIVAL OF LEARNING

Another important development contributed to the gradual breakdown of the Holy Roman Empire: the *Renaissance* or the *Revival of Learning* in which much useful knowledge of the ancient Greeks was rediscovered and disseminated among scholars. Although this movement became increasingly centered on man and his intellectual and scientific abilities, not all those individuals involved were anti-religious, nor were its discoveries unimportant.

In his "Hand of God in American History," (*Consider and Ponder,* pp. 46–54) Rev. S. J. Foljambe portrays this movement as also a part of Divine Providence. It was, he explains, the capture of Constantinople by the Turks in 1453 "which scattered the learning of the Greeks among the nations of the West." As this knowledge became widely known among European scholars, a spirit of inquiry was everywhere awakened, broader and freer than was ever known before. Then occurred the rediscovery of this continent [of North America], expanding the globe to the minds of the Old World, and stimulating a new spirit of enterprise and activity." (*Consider and Ponder,* p. 47)

INDIVIDUALS BEGAN TO CHALLENGE THE PHILOSOPHY OF THE ROMAN CHURCH

During the Revival of Learning, individuals began to challenge the philosophical basis of the Roman Church and the entire medieval system of learning that was based largely on the ideas of one of the ancients — Aristotle — and consisted of deducing conclusions from his philosophical premises as established by the Church.

Among the first of these individuals who challenged the medieval foundation of learning was Roger Bacon (1214–1294) an English Franciscan friar renowned for his discoveries in mathematics, chemistry and the mechanic arts.

Note, however, that Bacon, like other scientific minds who followed him, was not rebelling against the Scriptures but, rather, against the medieval Church's closed system of learning which did not allow for new discoveries in God's world.

THE TRUE FUNCTION OF PHILOSOPHY

"In Part II of [Roger Bacon's] 'Opus Majus,' in which he discusses the relation between theology and philosophy, he claims that all truth is to be found in the sacred Scriptures and that it is the function of philosophy to trace our knowledge of natural things back to the principles contained in these." (John W. Burgess, *The Sanctity of Law,* Boston (1927), p. 71)

Note also Bacon's comments on page 174 of your text, that "God has not created the world for the sake of the universal man, but for the sake of individual persons...."

In your reading assignment, historian Burgess discusses some of the outstanding individuals of the 15th, 16th and 17th centuries who began the birth of modern science: Copernicus (1475–1543), the great Polish astronomer; Galileo Galilei (1564–1642), Italian astronomer and physicist; Johannes Kepler (1571–1630), German astronomer; Baron von Leibnitz (1646–1716), German philosopher; and England's Sir Isaac Newton (1642–1727), natural scientist and discoverer of the law of gravitation.

The great men who appeared at this time in every field were, says Rev. Foljambe, "both the ripe fruit and the creators of their times.... They are God's gift to the world, and in their thought and work indicate the world's progress, and are its means and helpers." (*Consider and Ponder*, p. 48)

These individuals used their God-given ability to reason and discover new truths about God's world. Alfred North Whitehead (1861–1947), a distinguished mathematician, calls Christianity the mother of science because these early scientific minds recognized the universe as one of order proceeding according to the laws laid down by the Creator. They believed, says Whitehead, "that every detailed occurrence can be correlated with its antecedents in a perfectly definite manner, exemplifying general principles." (See "The Rise of Modern Science" in Francis Schaeffer, *How Shall We Then Live?* p. 133)

A NEW WORLD IN THEOLOGY

Rev. Foljambe declared that these individuals had a providential place and purpose in history. But he acknowledged that not all their discoveries or even the wonderful discovery of the New World "had aroused such mighty energy in the mind of Christendom as did the discovery of a new world in theology by Luther, and the sudden reformation in religion which sprung up in Germany, and swiftly extended through Northern Europe." (*Consider and Ponder*, p. 47) This "new world in theology" was based upon *The Bible, rather than the Church, as the supreme authority* to govern all areas of life and upon the *right of individual conscience* to interpret the Scriptures with the aid of the Holy Spirit. As they read the Bible, individuals also began to question the form of government of the Church and its relation to the state.

A great impetus was given to the search for the sanctity of law and the development of the individual's God-given capacities under the authority of his revealed Word, as the Reformers gave the Bible to the people in their own languages for that they might interpret it for themselves and interpret all things in the light of Scripture. (See *T & L*, pp. 168–172 for details on the work of the great Reformers, Martin Luther and John Calvin. You will also be studying more about the Reformation in Step Five of this lesson.)

Now proceed with your Reading Assignment for Step Two, which is to read on "Law" and "What is the State?" on pp. 140–142; "Sanctity of Law and the Renaissance," pp. 173–176; and "Individual Man Encounters the Church-State," pp. 177–183.

STEP THREE:
QUESTIONS FOR INVENTION

1. After reading the definitions of "law" on p. 140 of your text, how would you define law?

2. How does a rule of civil conduct laid down by the supreme power in a state differ from a rule of conduct laid down by the church or a private philosopher or teacher of ethics? (See *Union*, p. 143)

3. What gives laws their sanction and how does the "sanction of law" differ from the "sanctity of law"? (See *Union*, p. 146)

4. After reading the definitions of "the state" on pp. 141–142, define the state in your own words.

5. Francis Lieber was one of America's first political scientists. According to him, why does the state exist? Does it exist to protect the rights of the majority? Minorities against the majority? Or the individual? (See Lieber quote in *Union*, p. 141)

6. Lieber wrote in the late nineteenth century. What English Christian cleric of the 13th century spoke in similar terms concerning the individual and what did he say? (See *Union*, pp. 173–174)

7. Upon the ideas of what Greek philosopher was medieval philosophy largely based? (See *Union*, p. 175)

8. Why were Roger Bacon, Copernicus, Galileo, and other great scientists persecuted by the Roman Church? (See *Union*, p. 182)

9. Why were Leibnitz and Newton not persecuted by the civil authorities in their countries? (See *Union*, pp. 182–183)

10. Were the founders of modern science hostile to Christianity or did they find the inspiration for their research in their religion? Explain.

STEP FOUR:

FURTHER STUDY OF PRINCIPLES AND LEADING IDEAS

To understand better the development of the Roman Republic which was of great interest to our forefathers, see the chart, *The Development of the Roman Republic,* on the following page, and the chart on the next following page, *The Decline of the Roman Republic.*

After studying these two charts, read the material in Burgess on "Emergence of Christian Communities," pp. 147–152.

Note his comments on the *class basis* of representation in the governmental bodies of the Roman Republic. (See particularly p. 149, first paragraph)

It was under the system described by Professor Burgess, at least theoretically, that Rome conquered the world. In fact, however, it was really the senate of the patricians with their consuls and other officers, together with the military commanders, who carried on 150 years of conquest, while the tribunes of the people and their assembly "kept quiet." It was, however, *a system that promoted collision between the classes* since the representatives of the common people (Plebians) were represented by a separate assembly from that of the aristocrats (Patricians) who held the greatest political power. This state of affairs ultimated in rebellion and increasing anarchy, until a "strong man" appeared in the person of Julius Caesar, and the republic gradually began to change its character.

Note that, even in its best days, Rome's conquered peoples, though incorporated into Roman life and given the protection of Roman law, were not represented at all in the Roman government. (See *Christian History,* Vol. I, p. 13)

The first Roman emperor, Octavian (who ruled as Augustus Caesar), and was a nephew of the slain Julius Caesar, did not immediately seize all power and abolish the Roman senate. According to historian Edward Gibbon, "it was on the dignity of the senate that Augustus and his successors founded their new empire; and they affected on every occasion, to adopt the language and principles of Patricians. In the administrations of their powers they frequently consulted the great national council [the senate], and seemed to refer to its decisions the most important concerns of peace and war." (Edward Gibbon, *The Decline and Fall of the Roman Empire,* Vol. I, Chapter III, p. 60)

But finally the Senate was "respectfully suffered to sink into oblivion... [and] was left a venerable but useless monument of antiquity on the Capitoline hill." (*Ibid.,* Chapter VIII, pp. 329–330)

As you consider the material you have read here and in your reading assignment thus far, answer the following questions:

1. Was representation in the Roman Republic based on the individual or on the class to which he belonged? (See *Union,* pp. 148–149 and the chart on the next page of this *Guide* on *The Development of the Roman Republic*)

2. What kind of conflict did this method of representation cause?

3. When Octavian became emperor, did he *immediately* centralize all power in his person?

4. Has our American system of government been altered in one or two great sweeping steps?

Now read pp. 153–173 of your text. Note the shift in power from the Emperor to the Pope in the Holy Roman Empire. After you have read these selections, answer the following questions:

1. What was the fundamental principle of the new Church-State of the Holy Roman Empire? (See *Union,* p. 160)

2. Under this system who or what gave sanction to the laws of the Emperor? The Bible, the traditions of the Christian Church, or the Pope? (See *Union,* p. 160)

3. What happened to the sanctity of law when Charlemagne divided the Empire between his sons? (See *Union,* p. 169, par. 2 & 3)

4. In converting peoples, like the English, for example, did the Roman Church start a great missionary endeavor to reach them as individuals, or did the Church concentrate on converting the leaders? Which method do you think most accords with Christianity? (See *Union,* p. 171)

5. What kind of Christians do you have when the people simply follow their leaders into the Church *by necessity* rather than by individual *choice?*

STEP FIVE:

ORIGINAL THOUGHT

In your Reading Assignment for Step Two, you studied some outstanding individuals in the field of

DEVELOPMENT OF THE ROMAN REPUBLIC

For when the Gentiles, which have not the law, do by nature the things contained in the law, these, having not the law, are a law unto themselves: which shew the work of the law written in their hearts, their conscience also bearing witness, and their thoughts the mean while accusing or else excusing one another. (Romans 2:14-15)

The Roman Republic was the best attempt of the pagan world to develop representative government and a written civil code without the aid of divine revelation in the Holy Scriptures.

1. Tribes known as Latins settled in the middle peninsula of Southern Europe (800–750 B.C.). Their territory, barely 30 by 40 miles, was called Latium.

2. Their government: (See *Union*, pp. 147–148) By a tribal chief and

   (1) *A Council of Elders* (origin of Roman *Senate*, from *L.* "*senex*," meaning "old") consisting of fathers of families.

   (2) *A Council of All Adult Males* (origin of the *Comitia Curiata*) Made up of groups of families, each group known as a "curia," and each curia's vote counting as one vote.

   The Role of Each Council: To protect its members against injustice from the Chief.

3. 750–500 B.C., Latium was conquered and ruled by Etruscan kings with the Senate and Comitia Curiata.

4. *Comitia Centuriata* was formed because of growth of population outside city. It consisted of all arms bearing men both within and without the city. It assembled in time of war by hundreds or "centuries" but this body soon became dominated by nobles who robbed the *Comitia Curiata* of power.

5. The *Plebians* (common people) demanded a greater share in government and revolted in 493 B.C. *Tribunes* were elected from the people to represent their interests: 2 at first, then 10. (in 471 B.C., they became a separate assembly, the *Comitia Tributa.* (See *Union*, p. 148)

6. In 500 B.C. the people ousted the Etruscan kings.

7. But the nobility (*Patricians*) had the main power in their *Senate*. They elected *two consuls* as heads of state to rule for one year only. (The senators served for life.)

8. The *Tribunes* had only veto power over laws of the Senate. They could not become consuls or hold other top positions. Only patricians could serve as consuls, judges, army generals, heads of the treasury, etc. (See *Union*, pp. 148–149)

9. The *Tribunes* could approve or disapprove a law but could not propose laws. They could only vote on laws submitted to them by the Senate.

10. *Tribunes* and *Patricians* demanded written laws to clarify the bounds of their powers. (See *Union*, p. 148)

11. In 450 B.C., Roman Law was engraved on 12 tablets of bronze. (See page 148.)

12. Gradually, over a period of two centuries, the people gained the rights they desired: A *Tribune* was elected to the Senate (376 B.C.), and *plebians* began to hold other top positions (337 B.C.)

13. But the character of the Roman Republic was radically altered as Rome became a world power burdened with the government of many other peoples.

SOURCES: *Christian History of the Constitution,* Vol. II, Christian Self-Government with Union, compiled by Verna M. Hall; *Ancient Times, A History of the Early World,* by James Henry Breasted

science who opposed the medieval Church-State of the Holy Roman Empire. Now you will be reading about the outstanding religious reformers of the Reformation beginning with John Wycliffe, "the morning Star of the Reformation"; then Martin Luther, Ulrich Swingli, John Calvin, and others. (Read pp. 185–196 of your text on "The One Church-State Empire Expands to Many National Church-States")

"I WILL HARRY THEM OUT OF THE LAND. . . ."

Continue reading on the religious conflicts in Great Britain between James I and his son Charles I and English and Scottish Calvinists (pp. 197–208). Recollect that James I (1566–1625), like his predecessor, Elizabeth I (1533–1603), opposed both the Puritans who were trying to reform the English Church from within and the Separatists who had left the official state church and claimed the right to form their own churches by covenant. The Pilgrims, who were Separatists, suffered persecution and imprisonment. Indeed, James I warned all dissenters from the English Church that he would "harry them out of the land, or else do worse."

"NO BISHOP, NO KING"

Note that James I, though raised by Calvinists at his Scottish Court, became enamoured of the Episcopal form of government when he became King of England. (See the Mosheim quote on page 197 of your text that brings out the distaste James felt for anything like "a republic, synod or council.")

At the Hampton Court Conference of 1604, James declared that a Scots presbytery "agrees with monarchy as well as God and the devil; then Jack and Tom, Will and Dick shall meet, and at their pleasure censure me and my council. . . ." (See *Union,* p. 201) He told the bishops that if the Puritans were in their place, "I know what would become of my supremacy, for, NO BISHOP, NO KING." (*Ibid.*) He obviously believed that what gave legitimacy — or sanctity — to his rule was the anointing of the Bishop in his coronation.

THE DIVINE RIGHT OF KINGS

As the Roman Emperors had attempted to give sanctity to their laws by claiming to be divine, so now James I claimed that he ruled by divine right. He elaborated his "Divine Right of Kings" theory of government in his treatise: "The True Law of Free Monarchy." Englishmen were familiar with the claim made by their Tudor monarch, Henry VIII, that he ruled as "an absolute king." But by this Henry meant a king who was independent of all foreign or papal influence, as indeed Henry VIII was when he broke with the Church of Rome and made himself head of the Church of England.

"James I chose to regard the words as implying the monarch's freedom from all control by law, or from responsibility to anything but his own royal will." (John Richard Green, *A Short History of the English People,* p. 478) James even went so far as to declare in a speech: "As it is atheism and blasphemy to dispute what God can do, so it is presumption and a high contempt in a subject to dispute what a king can do, or to say that a king cannot do this or that." (*Ibid.*)

THE TEMPER OF THE PURITAN

This Divine Right of Kings theory of James I collided head on with the views of the Puritans who were close students of the Bible. English historian John Richard Green writes in his *Short History of the English People,* p. 479:

"The temper of the Puritan was eminently a temper of law. The diligence with which he searched the Scriptures sprang from his earnestness to discover a Divine Will which in all things, great or small, he might implicitly obey. But this implicit obedience was reserved for the Divine Will alone, *for human ordinances derived their strength only from their correspondence with the revealed law of God.* The Puritan was bound by his very religion to examine every claim made on his civil and spiritual obedience by the powers that be; and to own or reject the claim, as it accorded with the higher duty which he owed to God."

THE SOLEMN LEAGUE AND COVENANT

As you read your text, note that Charles I (1600–1649), son of James I, obstinately tried to continue his father's plan to force the Episcopal form of government on the Scottish Kirk, but that the Scots promptly drew up the Solemn League and Covenant, formed themselves into an army, and marched into England in 1640. To Charles I's consternation, the English Parliament supported the Scottish patriots. Thus began the English Civil War from which the leader of the Parliamentary army, Oliver Cromwell, rose to be the leader of the nation after the execution of Charles I on January 30, 1649.

Impatient with the dissension between different factions in the Parliament as to what form of government should be adopted to replace the monarchy, Cromwell dissolved it (in 1653) and summoned a new Parliament under the control of the army. This Parliament then elected him to rule as Lord Protector of England.

DECLINE OF THE ROMAN REPUBLIC

For the wrath of God is revealed from heaven against all ungodliness and unrighteousness of men, who hold the truth in unrighteousness; because that which may be known of God is manifest in them; for God hath shewed it unto them. (Romans 1:18-19)

This chart shows that, as Roman virtue declined, so did the Roman Republic, which finally degenerated into a military dictatorship.

1. Between 500–275 B.C., the tiny Roman Republic on the Tiber conquered all of the Italian Peninsula south of the Po Valley. Their only rival was Carthage.

2. Carthage was finally defeated in 201 B.C.

3. But Rome failed to govern its conquered provinces properly.
   - It accorded only partial citizenship to the inhabitants of these provinces:
     – It protected their right to carry on business and commerce;
     – gave them Roman rights in civil courts of law;
     – accorded some social privileges, *i.e.*, the right to intermarry with Romans.
   - But citizenship *did not* include voting rights.
   - Roman governors were absolute rulers in the conquered provinces, which they looted for their personal profit as well as for Rome's coffers.

4. Rome grew rich from her conquered provinces.
   - The governors of conquered provinces returned to Rome wealthy men while ordinary soldiers came home to poverty. (See *Union*, p. 150)
   - Roman virtue declined; luxury and vice abounded.
   - Some wealthy Romans bought up farms of poor men. (Soldiers, for example, returned from war to find their farms sold for debt.)

5. Wealthy Romans used slaves to work their big landholdings.

6. Penniless soldiers gave up farming and returned to the army or drifted into the city to live on free "bread and circuses."

7. Other small farmers were forced to sell their holdings because of competition of cheap grains that were imported from Egypt and Africa which the Roman government often gave away free.

8. The Gracchus brothers, Tiberius, elected a Tribune in 133 B.C., and Gaius, elected Tribune in 123, tried to get some public lands given to poor farmers, but both were murdered, Tiberius by a mob of senators and Gaius in a street riot. (See Burgess, *Union*, p. 149)

9. A century of civil turmoil followed (133-31 B.C.), during which Romans, torn by class warfare, turned to their military leaders for protection from growing anarchy.

10. Rome finally succumbed to the military dictatorship of its greatest hero, Julius Caesar, conqueror of most of the Mediterranean world. (See Burgess, *Union*, p. 149)

11. Caesar was assassinated in the Senate in 44 B.C.

12. His nephew, Octavius, gained complete power in 31 B.C., and was subsequently made Caesar Augustus and Imperator (Commander), a title more acceptable to the people than that of king.

13. Caesar Augustus *appeared* to defer to the senate but had the real power in his hands with the backing of the army. He consolidated his empire and by 30 B.C. the entire Mediterranean world was under control of the Roman Empire.

SOURCES: *Christian History of the Constitution*, Vol. II, Christian Self-Government with Union, compiled by Verna M. Hall; *Ancient Times, A History of the Early World*, by James Henry Breasted

Note that, as the authority of the Pope over England had been repudiated by Henry VIII, so now Englishmen had repudiated the assumption of James I and Charles I that the monarchy was the vehicle through which God made His will known for the government of men. *No longer did a king give the laws of the land their sanctity and power.* The power to determine the sanctity of law now shifted to the House of Commons as the representative of the English people. Now it was "the reason and conscience of those representatives in their interpretation of truth, right, and policy" which was to have "the compelling force of law" over the minds of Englishmen." (See p. 208 of your text)

ENGLAND REVERTS TO MONARCHICAL GOVERNMENT

But the English experiment with republicanism of a sort was brief and was virtually ended when Oliver Cromwell dissolved Parliament in 1653. Cromwell's contributions as a statesman, however, were admirable in many ways:

"For five years now he pursued with great success the work of consolidating England, Scotland, and Ireland into one national state; and in giving the British Commonwealth such an international standing as it had never before enjoyed; and at the end of his life so pre-eminent was his popularity and prestige that his son Richard succeeded him without any opposition worth noting." (*Union*, pp. 206–207)

But soon opposition began to develop to Richard Cromwell. Many Englishmen were tired of the arbitrary rule of a military dictatorship which stifled all dissent. They believed it would be better to return to the old rule of King and Parliament. At least under this system, they reasoned, they would have some say in the government through freely elected representatives. So England reverted to the monarchical system under Charles II.

During his reign, there was a great exodus of Puritans from England because of intense persecution by the Anglican Church. The Bishops resisted the attempts of the Puritans to discard rituals and ceremonies they viewed as unbiblical and to make the sermon the focus of the church service. The Archbishop of Canterbury was supported by Charles II in his attempt to purge the Church of Puritan pastors and force the English people to conform to the state church. New England was now to be the theater for the greater development of Christian self-government and union.

Read "The United States of America," in your text, pp. 209–211 and "Three Centuries of Thought and Action" on pp. 211–212.

Consider the reason for the confidence of the Pilgrims that they could establish a body politic in the New World to the glory of God and advancement of the Christian faith. They had a textbook to guide them: The Bible.

THE BIBLE: SOURCE OF THE SANCTITY OF LAW

Having the Bible in their own language, led all of the peoples of Christendom to rethink their lives and relationships so that they might square with the teachings of Scripture.

- John Wycliffe (c. 1320–1384) translated the Bible into the English vernacular more than 100 years before the Great Reformation thus laying the foundation for reform of both Church and State. (See *Union*, pp. 185–186)

- Martin Luther (1482–1546) accepted the Bible as divine revelation, "but it was *the Bible as understood and interpreted by each [individual] for himself,* and not as handed down to him by Pope or curia, bishop or council." (See your text, p. 190) Luther translated the Bible into German enriching the German language in the process. (See *Union*, p. 191)

- John Calvin (1509–1564), French Protestant theologian, was called to reform the Swiss city of Geneva. He translated the Bible into French and emphasized the sovereignty of God and the authority of the Scriptures. (See *Union*, p. 193–194)

Read also about these three men in *T & L* on pp. 166–172. Then write an essay on one of them showing how his ideas played an important role in developing the Christian idea of the sanctity of law.

STEP SIX:

WHAT CHRISTIAN PRINCIPLES AND IDEAS IDENTIFY THE AMERICAN POLITICAL UNION?

1. The American idea of sanctity of law differed from the European which placed it in Emperor, Pope or King. In America, where the Gospel Law took root, *sanctity of law was found in the Bible as understood by the God-governed individual.* (See *Union*, pp. 209–210) Americans believed with Richard Hooker that "Of Law, no less can be said, than that her seat is the bosom of God, her voice the harmony of the world." (*Union*, p. 140)

2. Three distinguished Americans have defined the state as:

- "...a complete body of free persons, united together for their common benefit, to enjoy peaceably what is their own, and to do justice to others" (James Wilson);

- "...a society of moral beings [which] exists for the better obtaining of the true ends of each individual and of society collectively" and which "does not make right, but is founded upon it" (Francis Lieber);

- "...a body politic, or civil society of men, united together to promote their mutual safety and prosperity by means of their union." (Samuel Adams) (See *Union*, pp. 141–142)

3. The formation of the American states and then the union of those states into one nation was effected by means different from those employed in the Old World (by force and conquest). In America union developed voluntarily from the family, the congregation, the community and the individual states. (See *Union*, p. 211)

4. Under the American union, "The rights of a State are defined by the Constitution, and cannot be invaded without violation of it...." (Alexander Hamilton) and "The State governments may be regarded as constituent and essential parts of the federal government; whilst the latter is nowise essential to the operation or organization of the former. ... The powers delegated by the proposed Constitution to the federal government are few and defined. Those which are to remain in the State governments are numerous and indefinite." (James Madison) (*Union*, p. 142)

LESSON SIX

THE NATION AND THE LAW OF NATURE

*For when the Gentiles, which have not the law, do by nature
the things contained in the law, these, having not the law, are a law unto themselves:
Which shew the work of the law written in their hearts, their conscience also bearing witness,
and their thoughts the mean while accusing or else excusing one another.*
(Romans 2:14–15)

As you have learned (in Lesson Two), our Founding Fathers were concerned about establishing proper relations with other nations based on the Law of Nations, which, in turn, was seen as resting on God's moral law inclusive of the Law of Nature written in men's hearts and confirmed in the Scriptures. They studied the writings of William Blackstone who maintained that the precepts in the Bible "are found upon comparison to be really a part of the original law of nature, as they tend in all their consequences to man's felicity." (See *Christian History,* Vol. I, p. 143)

Writers on the Law of Nature generally agreed that it was impossible, however, for sinful man to understand the Law of Nature in its full extent and intent without the aid of divine Revelation. John Locke, in discussing the inadequacy of human reason to discover the Law of Nature in its entirety, wrote that "'tis plain in Fact, that human Reason unassisted, failed Men in its great and proper business of Morality. It never from unquestionable Principles, by clear Deductions, made out an entire Body of the Law of Nature.... But such a Body of Ethicks, proved to be the Law of Nature, from Principles of Reason, and reaching all the Duties of Life; I think no Body will say the World had before our Saviour's time." (*Union,* p. 217)

In this lesson you will learn more about the Law of Nature, particularly as it relates to the Law of Nations. You will also learn that prior to independence, our forefathers began to inquire about the Law of Nations as it related to the relationship between the American colonies and the Mother Country. There was much they needed to think through before they could be ready to consider independence.

During the ten-year period of constitutional debate between the colonies and the Mother Country (1765–1775), the colonists relied not only on their rights under the English Constitution, but also under the Law of Nature confirmed by Scriptural Law. They wrestled with such questions as: What constitutes the natural rights of a colony in connection with the Mother Country? To what extent do colonies of a nation possess the right to local self-government under the Law of Nations?

To answer these questions they studied works on the Law of Nations by such jurists as Hugo Grotius, Samuel de Puffendorf, and Emmerich de Vattel whose writings you will be studying in this lesson.

"The Rights of the British Colonies Asserted and Proved," by James Otis (see Step Five), is a good example of colonial reasoning on the Law of Nature and Nations as discussed by these jurists and applied by the Founding Fathers.

All of this study prepared Americans to declare their independence from the Mother Country and then to act in voluntary union throughout the War of

Independence. Over the ten-year period of debate with the Mother Country that preceded independence, Americans acquired a firm understanding of the "first principles" of righteous government and of the Christian character needed to be a self-governing people capable of working together in voluntary union.

They concurred with the English author, James Harrington, that "to make principles or fundamentals, belongs not to Men, to Nations nor to human Laws. To build upon such Principles or Fundamentals as are apparently laid by God in the inevitable Necessity or Law of Nature, is that which truly appertains to Men, to Nations, and to human Laws. To make any other Fundamentals, then build upon them, is to build Castles in the Air." (See *Union*, p. 216)

STEP ONE:
PRINCIPLES TO PONDER

1. THE LAW OF NATURE: AN ETERNAL RULE TO ALL MEN

"Thus the Law of Nature stands as an Eternal Rule to all Men, Legislators as well as others. The Rules that they make for other Men's Actions, must, as well as their own, and other Men's Actions, be conformable to the Law of Nature, *i.e.,* to the Will of God." (John Locke, *Union*, p. 221)

2. NATIONAL INDEPENDENCE IS A FUNDAMENTAL PRINCIPLE OF THE LAW OF NATIONS

"The law of nature . . . declares every nation free and independent of others." (Emmerich de Vattel, *Union*, p. 218)

". . . to assume among the Powers of the Earth, the separate and equal Station to which the Laws of Nature and of Nature's God entitle them. . . ." (The Declaration of Independence, July 4, 1776, *Union*, p. 215)

3. ACCORDING TO THE LAW OF NATURE, NATIONS HAVE A RIGHT TO SELF-DEFENSE

"To banish SELF-DEFENSE though pursued by FORCE, would be so far from promoting the Peace, that it would rather contribute to the Ruin and Destruction of Mankind. Nor is it to be imagin'd that the LAW OF NATURE, which was instituted for a Man's Security in the World, should favour so absurd a Peace, as must necessarily cause his present Destruction. . . ." (Samuel de Puffendorf, *Union*, p. 218)

STEP TWO:
READING FOR LEADING IDEAS

In your reading for Step Two, note the careful distinction that is made between the *nation* and the *state*. According to John W. Burgess, the *nation* is: "A population of an ethnic unity, inhabiting a territory of a geographic unity. . . ." It is also "a population having a common language and literature, a common tradition and history, a common custom and a common consciousness of rights and wrongs. . . ."

The *state*, on the other hand has a political and legal connotation. "Where the geographic and ethnic unities coincide, or very nearly coincide, the nation is almost sure to organize itself politically, — to become a state. . . . I trust it will be manifest to the mind of every reader how very important it is to distinguish clearly the nation, both in word and idea, from the state; preserving to the former its ethnic signification, and using the latter exclusively as a term of law and politics." (*Union*, p. 220)

THE NATIONAL STATE MUST PRECEDE THE WORLD STATE

Burgess also makes this profound comment: "The national state must be developed everywhere before the world-state can appear. . . . The state which attempts to realize . . . the world-order before the national-order, will find itself immediately threatened with dissolution and anarchy." (*Union*, p. 216)

In other words, world-order cannot be achieved until the nations of the world have individually mastered self-government in accord with God's revealed and natural laws and are united in supporting a Law of Nations that springs from those laws.

DEFINING THE LAW OF NATIONS

In Noah Webster's 1828 *American Dictionary of the English Language,* "the Law of Nations" is defined as "the rules that regulate the mutual intercourse of nations or states. These rules depend on the natural law, or the principles of justice which spring from the social state; or they are founded on customs, compacts, treaties, leagues and agreements between independent communities."

Webster also quotes American jurist James Kent: "By the law of nations we are to understand that code of public instruction, which defines the rights and prescribes the duties of nations, in their intercourse with each other."

As was alluded to in Lesson Two (Step Four), Hugo Grotius (1583–1645) was an eminent Dutch jurist whose great treatise, *The Laws of War and*

Peace, "produced a strong impression on the public mind of Christian Europe, and gradually wrought a most salutary change in the practical intercourse of nations in favor of humanity and justice." (*Union,* p. 22)

Many sovereigns of independent states became willing to bow to the moral rules of Grotius in the conduct of relations with other nations in peacetime and were even willing to be guided by them in the conduct of the war. Indeed, as American jurist Joseph Story described the application of the law of nature to the nations it showed them "the limits of lawful hostility; the mutual duties of belligerent and neutral powers" and, above all, it aimed "at the introduction into national affairs of that benign spirit of Christian virtue, which tempers the exercise even of acknowledged rights with mercy, humanity, and delicacy...." (*Union,* p. 299)

JAMES WILSON ON THE LAW OF NATURE AND NATIONS

James Wilson, eminent jurist and one of the framers of the Constitution, reflected the commonly accepted view of the Founding Father generation when he wrote "that the laws of morality are equally strict with regard to societies as to the individuals of whom the societies are composed." (*Union,* p. 222) It was his view that the Law of Nature which governed duties of individuals towards each other also governed the relations between states.

The Law of Nations begins with the duties the law of nature dictates to an individual. "Are there not duties he owes himself?" Wilson asks. "Is he not obliged to consult and promote his preservation, his freedom, his reputation, his improvement, his perfection, his happiness?" (*Ibid.*)

"Now that we see the law of nature as it respects the duties of individuals," he wrote, "let us see the law of nations as it respects the duties of states, to themselves: for we must recollect that *the law of nations is only the law of nature judicially applied to the conduct of states.*" (emphasis added) Thus, a state also "ought to attend to the preservation of its own existence." (*Ibid.*)

THE HAPPINESS OF NATIONS

Of what then does a state consist? "It consists in the association of the individuals of which it is composed.... It is the duty of a state, therefore, to preserve this association undissolved and unimpaired.... Nations, as well as men, are taught by the law of nature, gracious in its precepts, to consider their happiness as the great end of their existence. ..." (*Union,* pp. 222–223)

Wilson believed that in order to be happy, it was necessary "that the nation be instructed to search for happiness where happiness is to be found.... The education of youth, therefore, is of prime importance to the happiness of the state. The arts, the sciences, philosophy, virtue, and religion, all contribute to the happiness... of the nation. In this manner, public and private felicity will go hand in hand, and mutually assist each other in their progress...." (*Union,* p. 224)

THE DUTIES OF INDIVIDUALS AND NATIONS

Wilson believed also that nations, just like individuals, are not only forbidden to do evil, but are also commanded by the Law of Nature to do good to each other. "The duties of humanity are incumbent upon nations as well as upon individuals." (*Ibid.*)

An individual who has made a promise to another, is expected to fulfill that promise. Nations and their representatives are likewise expected, under the law of nations, "to preserve inviolably their treaties and engagements." Wilson was convinced that "In public as in private life, among sovereigns as among individuals, honesty is the best policy, as well as the soundest morality. Among merchants, credit is wealth; among states and princes, good faith is both respectability and power."

Wilson delivers this sharp warning on the consequences of an opposite policy: "A state, which violates the sacred faith of treaties, violates not only the voluntary, but also the natural and necessary law of nations, for we have seen that, by the law of nature, the fulfillment of promises is a duty as much incumbent upon states as upon men." (*Ibid.*)

TWO VIEWS OF THE LAWS OF NATIONS

Note that Wilson also makes an important distinction between the ideas of Grotius and Puffendorf on the Law of Nature and the Law of Nations, noting: "... we may here observe, that, with regard to the law of nations, Grotius and Puffendorf seem to have run into contrary extremes. The former was of opinion that the whole law of nations took its origin and authority from consent. The latter was of opinion, that every part of the law of nations was the same with the law of nature, that no part of it could receive its obligatory force from consent." (*Union,* p. 250)

Although Wilson agreed that the law of nations was a part of the law of nature, he cautioned: "Though the law of nations... be a part of the law of nature; though it spring from the same source; and though it is attended with the same obligatory power; yet it must be remembered that its application is made to very different objects. The law of nature is applied to individuals: the law of nations is applied to states." (*Union,* p. 238; see also Vattel, on p. 291)

Now proceed to your reading assignment in *Union*: on the Nation, pp. 215–216; The Nation and the Law of Nature, pp. 217–218; John W. Burgess on the state, p. 226. Then read the biography of Hugo Grotius, on pp. 239–241 of *Union,* his *Truths of the Christian Religion,* pp. 245–248, and the "Preliminary Discourse" to his *Rights of War and Peace,* pp. 252–262.

As you read the material on Grotius, consider that his *Rights of War and Peace* "was the first attempt to reduce into a system the subject of international law . . . before he wrote the ground was wholly unbroken." (*Union,* p. 244)

Note also that during the tumultuous theological debates between the Arminians and the Calvinists in the Netherlands, discussed on pp. 241–242, Grotius counselled "forebearance and mutual toleration." This accorded with his conviction, later expressed in his great work on the Law of Nations: "If all nations would submit to the law of CHRIST, and live up to it, whereunto there should nothing be wanting on God's Part; for it is certain, if all were Christians, and lived like Christians, there would be no wars. . . ." (*Union,* p. 19)

Step Three:
Questions for Invention

1. Explain the difference between a nation and a state.

2. According to Grotius, there is no excellence in the writing of the Greeks and the Hebrews that is not to be found in better form in "the law of Christ." Why is this so? (See *Union,* p. 246)

3. What are some of the "internal Principles" that God has implanted in man? and how have these Principles been made more clear and evident to us? (*Union,* p. 253)

4. From what foundation does Grotius derive civil laws, or civil government? (See par. XVI of his "Preliminary Discourse", *Union,* pp. 254–255)

5. Why is it Biblically wrong to believe that we may observe right and honor in our dealings within our own nation, but may disregard the dictates of right and honor in dealing with other nations?

6. Does the obligation of a nation to observe right

and justice toward another nation cease in time of war? (See par. XXVI, p. 256)

7. Does the Law of Nature and Nations require that no nation should go to war unless with a firm conviction of the justice of its cause? (See par. XXVIII, p. 257)

8. Is the Law of Nations binding upon a nation in the same way as the *internal* laws of a nation?

9. Is it likely that the moral power that lies in the Christian Law of Nations, as developed by Grotius, Puffendorf and others, would have the same weight with non-Christian and pagan nations? How should Christian nations deal with pagan nations in the field of international relations? Is it realistic to suppose that treaties entered into with such nations will be honored by them as of sacred obligation?

10. When the United States abrogates a long-standing treaty with a friendly nation in order to please the pagan government of a totalitarian nation, what does this tell other nations about our national character? And our character as individuals? (See James Wilson's comments in the last two paragraphs, *Union,* p. 224)

Step Four:
Further Study of Principles and Leading Ideas

For a deeper understanding of the Christian Law of Nature and Nations, read Barbeyrac's "Prefatory Discourse" to Puffendorf's *Law of Nature and Nations,* pp. 228–238. Then list in your notebook and answer the following questions:

1. Barbeyrac cites John Selden's book, *The Law of Nature and Nations, according to the Doctrine of the Hebrews.* Did Selden portray *all* Old Testament laws as part of the Law of Nature? (See *Union,* p. 231)

2. According to Barbeyrac, what did English philosopher and mathematician Thomas Hobbes (1588–1679) see as "the original cause of Civil Society"? (*Union,* p. 232)

3. How did Hobbes define the State of Nature and how does his definition differ from that of John Locke? (See *Union,* pp. 232, 217)

4. How much authority was Hobbes willing to

give to kings? And what was his attitude toward Christianity? (See Mosheim footnote in your text on p. 232)

Now read on Puffendorf, in your text, pp. 263–264, on "One Law," pp. 265, and Puffendorf's *Law of Nature and Nations,* pp. 266–286 and answer the following questions:

1. According to Puffendorf, what is the chief knowledge man needs in order to understand his duties towards himself and others? (*Union,* p. 270)

2. According to Puffendorf, does a Christian have the right of self-defense when assaulted by another person? (See *Union,* pp. 272–273)

3. How does Puffendorf interpret our Lord's commandment to love our neighbor as ourselves? Does Puffendorf believe our love for our neighbor should *exceed* our love for ourselves? (See p. 274)
And, in view of our Lord's Commandment to love others as ourselves, would there ever be an occasion when a nation would have the right to withhold goods from another in need of help? (See *Union,* p. 276)

4. In Puffendorf's opinion, what is necessary to the creation of a Commonwealth, or Civil State? (See *Union,* pp. 283–284)

5. Puffendorf distinguishes between two kinds of union, when "two or more States are subject to one and the same King" and "when two or more States are link'd together in one Body by virtue of some League or Alliance."
In the latter case, how can such states more closely unite into an actual civil state, rather than continue as a loose league from which any state may withdraw at any time? Do you think what he had to say was of interest to the Founding Fathers when they sought to create "a more perfect union" under the United States Constitution? (See *Union,* p. 285)

Now read Emmerich de Vattel's *The Law of Nations or Principles of the Law of Nature* in your text, pp. 288–298 and Justice Joseph Story's comments on studying the Law of Nations, pp. 299–300. (NOTE: Joseph Story (1779–1845) was a prominent Massachusetts lawyer who was appointed to the United States Supreme Court in 1811 where he served for more than 30 years. In 1828 he also became a professor of law at Harvard University. His 12-volume *Commentaries on the Constitution of the United States,* an authoritative treatment of American consti-

tutional law, were drawn from the courses he gave at Harvard.)

1. Why did Emmerich de Vattel believe that nations are "as so many free persons living together in the state of nature?" (See *Union,* p. 290)

2. According to Vattel, how can we understand the two fundamental obligations of nations? (See *Union,* p. 291)

3. How did Vattel believe we could distinguish between lawful and unlawful treaties between nations? (See pp. 291–292)

4. In addition to the original law of nations rooted in the Christian Law of Nature, Vattel introduces another kind of law of nations. Describe this second law of nations.

5. What did Justice Story say was the duty of all "who aspire to be statesmen"? (See *Union,* p. 299)

6. Why did he believe that the principles of natural law were as applicable to individual nations as to individual persons? (See *Union,* p. 299)

7. What did he believe was needed in order to temper a nation's exercise of its acknowledged rights? (See p. 299)

STEP FIVE:
ORIGINAL THOUGHT

Turn to p. 380 of your text and read *The Rights of the British Colonies Asserted and Proved* (1764) by James Otis, Boston lawyer and patriot.

As you read his paper, consider the historical background that led to its writing. Jedediah Morse tells us (p. 351) that the Mother Country had allowed the colonists to tax themselves for a century and a half beginning with the establishment of the colonies. Great Britain did restrain and regulate their trade, however, and prohibited the colonies from manufacturing many articles which it was believed would injure England's manufacturing industries. (See *Union,* p. 351)

LOCAL AND GENERAL CONCERNS OF THE COLONIES

Morse also makes this most significant observation: "The filial submission of the colonies to the sovereignty of the parent country, for so long a period, while it was exercised in superintending their *general concerns,* and in harmonizing the commercial interests of the empire, gave a clear demonstration, that, without parliamentary taxation, they might have been kept in proper subordination and subserviency to her government and interests." (See *Union,* p. 352)

Great Britain had unwittingly allowed a kind of *de facto* right of local self-government to develop even though it was at odds with the English theory of Empire, *i.e.,* that Parliament had the right to legislate for the colonies if it wished to do so. Because Americans had enjoyed a large degree of local self-government *in practice,* over a period of 150 years, they came to believe that they had the right of self-government in regard to their *local concerns.*

THE FIRST FAINT OUTLINES OF AMERICAN FEDERAL THEORY

In this view, so ably presented in the paper by James Otis, may be seen the first faint outlines of what was to develop in the future as American *federal theory.* To be sure, at this point in the development of the idea of federal union, Otis conceived of the place of the colonies in the Empire as similar to the position today of the various nations that compose the British Commonwealth of Nations, *i.e., a loose league of self-governing nations* which are *united in some matters of general concern,* such as economic and trade policy but which are *in other respects independent, and self-governing.* (Today, the countries comprising the British Commonwealth of Nations are completely independent with regard to their political decisions. Thus, they do not constitute a federal union such as ours where there are two kinds of sovereignty operating on the same people, but within different spheres. The Governor General of Canada, for example, is only a courtesy title for the representative of Great Britain, and the English Parliament has no authority over the Canadian federal government or the provincial legislatures.)

GROUNDS OF COLONIAL RIGHTS

At the time of the Stamp Act, when Otis was penning his paper, the view was prevalent that the colonies could claim the right of self-government from the English Constitution as well as from the Law of Nature and Nations as outlined by such writers as Locke, Grotius, Puffendorf and Vattel. The patriot leaders believed, therefore, that political authority over the colonists should not be concentrated in the Parliament of Great Britain three thousand miles away, a government in which they had no representatives. Theirs was a doctrine of *dispersed* not *concentrated* powers — which is the very essence

of American federalism. They were convinced that governmental powers should be carefully differentiated between those properly belonging to the Mother Country and those properly belonging to the colonies.

Otis criticizes Grotius and Puffendorf for describing the relationship of colonies to their parent countries in merely factual terms rather than discussing the philosophical reasons why these relationships existed. But he quotes a passage from Puffendorf (on page 382 of your text) which points toward eventual independence of a colony from the parent country:

"Different commonwealths may be formed out of one by common consent, by sending out colonies in the manner usual in Old Greece. For the Romans afterwards when they sent a colony abroad, continued it under the jurisdiction of the mother commonwealth, or greater country. But the colonies planted by the Greeks, and after their method, *constituted particular commonwealths,* which were obliged only to pay a kind of deference and dutiful submission to the mother commonwealth." (emphasis added)

Note also the statement Otis makes which, in effect, summarizes his position on the right relationship that should exist between the colonies and the Mother Country. (See last paragraph of the extracts from *The Rights of the Colonies,* page 391) Note, too, the definition he gives of this relationship in the first two paragraphs of the letter to the London agent for Massachusetts. (See p. 366 of your text)

Write a short paper on these first steps toward American federal theory, *i.e.,* toward the idea of two spheres of government over the same people — one to handle their *general concerns* and the other their *local concerns.* Consider and answer these questions in your essay: What has been the result of Americans forgetting their unique "dual form of government" with sovereignty divided between the states and the nation? Who is responsible for restoring the constitutional balance between these two spheres of government — the state governments, the United States Congress, or the American people?

STEP SIX:

WHAT CHRISTIAN PRINCIPLES AND IDEAS IDENTIFY THE AMERICAN POLITICAL UNION?

1. *The Founding Fathers studied God's Law of Nature as applied to the Law of Nations.* The Founding Fathers studied closely the writings of Grotius, Puffendorf, Vattel, Locke and other Christian writers

on God's Law of Nature as applied to relations between nations. Alexander Hamilton once urged a political opponent to "apply yourself without delay to the study of the law of nature. I would recommend to your perusal, Grotius, Puffendorf, Locke...." (*Union,* p. 250)

2. *The Law of nations was seen as part of God's moral law.* These authors saw the Law of Nations as a part of God's moral law revealed in His Word or in His Law of Nature. "The obligations of the Law of Nature, cease not in Society, but only in many Cases are drawn closer, and have by human Laws known Penalties annexed to them, to inforce their Observation. Thus the Law of Nature stands as an Eternal Rule to all Men, Legislators, as well as others. The Rules that they make for other Men's actions, must, as well as their own, and other Men's Actions, be conformable to the Law of Nature, *i.e.,* to the Will of God...." (John Locke, *Union,* p. 287)

"We must then apply to nations the rules of the law of nature, in order to discover what are their obligations, and what are their laws; consequently the law of nations is originally no more than *the law of nature applied to nations."* (Emmerich de Vattel, *Union,* p. 291)

3. *James Otis claimed The Rights of Colonies under the Law of Nations.* Prior to the War of Independence, during the decade of debate with the Mother Country (1765–1775), the Founding Fathers were particularly concerned about the rights of colonies in relation to their mother countries under the Law of Nations. In an important paper, *The Rights of the Colonies Asserted and Proved,* Boston patriot James Otis wrote: "The Colonists are by the law of nature free born, as indeed, all men are, white or black.... The Colonists being men, have a right to be considered as equally entitled to all the rights of nature with the Europeans.... By being or becoming members of society, they have not renounced their natural liberty in any greater degree than any other good citizens, and if tis taken from them without their consent, they are so far enslaved." (pp. 383–384)

4. *His paper was an early statement of federal theory.* Otis believed that the colonies should be represented in parliament "in some proportion to their number and estates...." Thus, he saw the British Empire as a kind of grand confederation of largely self-governing states. (See *Union,* p. 391) His paper was an early statement of federal theory within the Empire.

5. *The colonies were led to claim full independence from the Mother Country.* But Great Britain continued to claim a right to tax and rule the colonies arbitrarily without their own consent. This made full, not partial independence from Great Britain desirable and, indeed, inevitable. Here, too, the Founding Fathers were guided by the Law of Nations "to assume among the Powers of the Earth, the separate and equal Station to which the Laws of Nature's God entitle them...." (Thomas Jefferson, *The Declaration of Independence,* p. 215)

Emmerich de Vattel, like the other writers on the Law of Nations which the founders read so closely, declared that nations were "free and independent of each other, in the same manner as men are naturally free and independent.... Each nation ought to be left in the peaceable enjoyment of that liberty it has derived from nature." (Vattel, p. 294)

6. *The Founding Fathers believed that national self-government must be founded on local self-government.* A proper union of states into a nation only arises when their local self-government is perfected under God's laws, revealed and natural. Jefferson wrote: "National self-government could not long endure except upon the foundation of local self-government.... It sustains and supports and keeps alive the whole fabric of the nation's political life." (p. 215)

LESSON SEVEN

PROVIDENTIAL STEPS TOWARD UNION

God that made the world and all things therein,
seeing that he is Lord of heaven and earth, dwelleth not in temples made with hands;
Neither is worshipped with men's hands, as though he needed any thing,
seeing he giveth to all life, and breath and all things;
And hath made of one blood all nations of men for to dwell on all the face of the earth,
and hath determined the times before appointed, and the bounds of their habitation.
(Acts 17:24–26)

This lesson discusses *four important providential steps* towards American union, the first of which you have already studied in some detail in Lesson 4.

1. The New England Confederacy — 1643
2. The New England Dominion (Great Britain's plan of colonial union) — 1688
3. William Penn's Plan of Union — 1698
4. The Albany Plan of Union — 1754

You will notice that the words *Divine Providence* and *providential* occur in Richard Frothingham's account of the developments leading to continental union. For example, there is this paragraph dealing with Benjamin Franklin's Albany Plan:

"This would have been not a mere league, but a self-sustaining government. The credit of this conception is due to the illustrious Franklin. It was original and American. . . . It is not strange that the form devised to carry it out should have been imperfect. The time had not ripened, the way had not been opened for such a stride in political science as a worthy embodiment of this ideal would have been. It required the discipline and the experience of the succeeding thirty years, the growth of a public opinion for a union, the rise of a sentiment of nationality, the possession of sovereignty, long training of the general mind in politics, and the wisdom of a cluster of

the peers of Franklin in intellect, before the conception could be embodied in a worthy form. *Divine Providence* permitted Franklin to share in this experience, to aid in forming the more perfect Union of the Constitution, and to see his countrymen establish it as the law of the land. . . ." (*Union,* pp. 332–333, emphasis added)

From this and other references to Divine Providence in relation to the history of the American Union, we can see that Frothingham held to *the providential view of history.*

Our forefathers believed that God intervenes in the lives of men and nations from time to time in order to fulfill His purposes and that history is moving in a straight line towards its triumphant close. (I Cor. 15:24–28)

According to Noah Webster's *American Dictionary of the English Language* (1828), Providence is "The care and superintendence which God exercises over his creatures. . . . A belief in divine providence is a source of great consolation to good men. By divine providence is understood God himself."

OUR FOUNDING FATHERS' FAITH IN DIVINE PROVIDENCE

The Founding Fathers believed so firmly in Divine Providence that *The Declaration of Indepen-*

dence concludes with the eloquent words: "And for the support of this Declaration, with a firm reliance on the protection of divine Providence, we mutually pledge to each other our lives, our fortunes, and our sacred honor." (*Union*, p. 26)

They were convinced that it was essential for men and nations to align themselves with the Divine Will in order to experience God's blessings. Hence, days of fasting and prayer were often proclaimed that the people might repent of their sins and turn to God for renewed guidance. Days of prayer and fasting were held in New England whenever confronted by a crisis (such as threatened invasion by the French in 1746). In Virginia in 1774, a day of prayer and fasting was proclaimed for the citizens of Boston when it was blockaded by Great Britain. The colonies together declared a Continental Fast Day on May 12, 1776, before Independence was declared. They also held days of Thanksgiving, such as that proclaimed by Congress at the end of the Revolutionary War:

"And whereas in the progress of a contest on which the most essential rights of human nature depended, the interpostion of Divine Providence in our favour hath been most abundantly and most graciously manifested, and the citizens of these United States have every reason for praise and gratitude to the God of their salvation. Impressed, therefore, with an exalted sense of the blessings by which we are surrounded, and of our entire dependence on that Almighty Being, from whose goodness and bounty they are derived, the United States in Congress assembled do recommend it to the several States, to set apart the second Thursday in December next, as a day of public thanksgiving...." (Cited by Verna M. Hall and Rosalie J. Slater in *The Bible and the Constitution*, p. 45)

George Washington, who had a deep faith in the rule of Divine Providence in his own life as well as that of the nation, often wrote of the intervention of Divine Providence during the War. He also saw the Hand of God in events leading to the "more perfect union" achieved by the United States Constitution.

"No people can be bound to acknowledge and adore the invisible hand which conducts the affairs of men more than the people of the United States. Every step by which they have advanced to the character of an independent nation seems to have been distinguished by some token of providential agency." (George Washington, *Union*, p. 337)

The providential view of history continued to be held well into the 19th century and is reflected in Rev. Foljambe's sermon, *The Hand of God in American History* in which he declared: "It has been said

that history is the biography of communities; in another, and profounder, sense, it is the autobiography of him 'who worketh all things after the counsel of his own will' (Ephesians 1:11), and who is graciously timing all events in the interests of His Christ, and of the Kingdom of God on earth." (See *Consider and Ponder*, p. 47)

STEP ONE:
PRINCIPLES TO PONDER

1. THE LOVE OF GOD AND MAN IS THE CHRISTIAN BOND OF UNION

"He gives them (the disciples) a bond of union, by which they should always be linked to him and to each other in the principle of love.... Here was the distinctive Mark, which all men would be able to read.... The apologists of the first centuries delighted in appealing to the common love of Christians, which was a new thing in the history of mankind.... By their love for each other, for mankind, for God, is it known or denied that men who call themselves Christians are really Christ's disciples." (W. H. Watkins, *Union*, p. 301)

2. WILLIAM PENN'S PLAN OF UNION WAS FOUNDED ON A SPIRIT OF FRATERNITY AND PATRIOTISM

"This plan recognized colonial customs, and is marked by the spirit of fraternity and patriotism, and by that aim in the common good which characterized the career of William Penn." (Richard Frothingham, *Union*, p. 323)

3. THE ALBANY PLAN PROPOSED A FORM OF UNION THAT PRESERVED THE PRINCIPLE OF LOCAL SELF-GOVERNMENT

"The Albany Plan was designed to establish for all America one government, based on the consent of the governed, and limited to general purposes, while it left to the local governments their separate functions." (Richard Frothingham, *Union*, p. 332)

4. THE AMERICAN UNION IS THE "PROVIDENTIAL PRODUCT" OF LOCAL SELF-GOVERNMENT

"This republic presents the rare and difficult system of one general government, the action of which extends over the whole nation, but which possesses certain enumerated powers, and of numerous State governments, which retain and exercise all powers not delegated to the Union.

".... A narrative of the rise of this system will show how instinctively the people appreciated and valued the grandest traditionary influence in all history, Local Self-government, and that providential product, American Union." (Richard Frothingham, *Union*, p. 306)

5. THE DUAL CITIZENSHIP OF AMERICANS IS A UNIQUE AMERICAN POLITICAL PRINCIPLE

"The People of the United States must be considered attentively in two very different views — as forming one nation, great and united; and as forming, at the same time, a number of separate states, to that nation subordinate, but independent as to their own interior government." (James Wilson, *Union*, p. 304)

STEP TWO:
READING FOR LEADING IDEAS

As you study the development of American unity and union in this lesson, recollect that "the first conception of an American union entertained by the founders of New England was to join in political bonds only those colonies in which the people were of a similar way of thinking in theology...." (See p. 304 of your text) Thus, the New England Confederacy (1643–1684) did not have a broad enough basis to include other colonies which did not share the same theological interpretation of the Scriptures. Nevertheless, as you saw in Lesson Four, it served a very useful purpose and was, in certain respects, a good example for the other colonies as further steps were taken to achieve colonial union.

THE DESIGNS OF CHARLES I
ON COLONIAL RIGHTS
ARE PROVIDENTIALLY THWARTED

Although Charles I (1600–1649) had planned far-reaching incursions on colonial rights by a major remodeling of their governments, he was providentially prevented from doing so. Because he was overthrown in the English Civil War, the New England Confederacy was allowed to continue for 41 years.

THE COMMONWEALTH UPHOLDS
COLONIAL RIGHTS TO
LOCAL SELF-GOVERNMENT

Under the Commonwealth government, led by Oliver Cromwell (1596–1658), there was no interference with the New England governments, although there were originally some designs in Parliament against the liberties of Massachusetts. But after receiving an eloquent appeal from the Massachusetts General Court for the continuation of their right to choose their own magistrates and make their own laws, these designs were dropped. (See *Christian History*, Vol. I, p. 282 and *Union*, p. 313)

CHARLES II OPPOSES
THE NEW ENGLAND CONFEDERACY

But when, after the death of Oliver Cromwell, the monarchy was restored and Charles II (1630–1685) ascended the throne in 1660, the Confederacy's days were numbered. The king was told that the colonies had formed the New England Confederacy with the express design "to throw off their dependence on England." (See *Union*, p. 13)

THE MASSACHUSETTS CHARTER IS ANNULLED

For some years the colonies were allowed to continue their internal government as before. But when Charles II had consolidated his power in England and had successfully canceled the charters and privileges of many English towns, he decided the time was ripe to dismantle the colonial governments by annulling their charters. He began in 1684 by canceling the Massachusetts Charter.

THE NEW ENGLAND DOMINION:
UNION UNDER A
CENTRALIZED ROYAL GOVERNMENT

It was his intention to bring *all* the colonies under one royal government headed by a general governor who would have absolute power over the colonial governments. His death in 1685 did nothing to reverse this policy, however, as his brother, James II (1633–1701), was even more absolutist in his views of the royal power and prerogative. In 1688, the New England colonies were officially joined with New York and New Jersey to form the New England Dominion and were put under the arbitrary rule of one man — Sir Edmund Andros — who was chosen by the king to exercise his royal policies in these colonies. Andros soon suspended all the colonists' time-honored rights.

"In all the colonies popular functions were absorbed by the Crown. It appointed local magistrates and county commissioners.... Town meetings for political purposes were either abrogated or restricted." (See *Union*, p. 315 for a discussion of violations of colonial rights in the other colonies.)

The Right to Self-Government is Partially Restored

Those incursions on the local self-government of the colonies were arrested and reversed when James II was forced into exile and the English people, in 1689, elected his daughter, Mary, and her husband, the Dutch Prince William of Orange, to rule as monarchs pledged to uphold the Constitution of England. The colonial charters were restored, although in Massachusetts the restoration was only partial, for the governor was now appointed by the King.

The Designs of France Produce Renewed Desire for Union

Note that a genuine union among the colonies became once again a pressing concern when the colonists were faced with the expansionist aims of France in America. (See *Union*, p. 316)

Note too, that after the 1690 massacre of the inhabitants of Schenectady by Indian allies of the French, the governor of Massachusetts urged united action for the defense of all the colonies and called for the first general congress of the colonies ever proposed.

William Penn's Plan of Union

In 1698 William Penn proposed a plan of union which would have created a colonial legislature with two delegates from each colony to legislate in matters of general concern. But, in the eyes of the colonies, the plan was flawed because of the mode of appointment of the presiding officer over the legislative body. (See *Union*, p. 323) London was not enthusiastic about the plan, either, and it was quietly shelved.

Keep in mind that, despite the resentment caused in the colonies by the New England Dominion, suggestions kept surfacing in London for uniting the colonies under the royal prerogative and that these efforts were supported in the colonies by the Tory Party. (See p. 324)

Now read pp. 303–308 of your text on "No Union Without Christian Self-Government"; pp. 314–321, "Schemes and Plans for a Union 1656 to 1754"; and from p. 322 to middle of p. 325.

Step Three:

Questions for Invention

1. Why did historian Frothingham call our American Union the Providential product of local self-government? (See *Union*, p. 306)

2. What idea of union, springing from "a deeply rooted conviction," was steadily pursued by "the popular party" in the colonies? (See *Union*, p. 306)

3. What was the governmental theory that Charles II tried to carry out in order to bring the colonies under one common government? (See *Union*, p. 315)

4. Describe the kind of colonial union that "the party of the prerogative" wanted to effect. How did it differ from that of "the popular party"? (See *Union*, pp. 324–325)

5. At what conference did the Northern and Southern colonies meet for the first time and what occasioned this meeting? (*Union*, p. 317)

6. What event prompted the governor of Massachusetts to call for a general congress of the colonies and how many colonies were involved in this congress? And what were the officers of the force raised to defend Albany required to do? (*Union*, p. 317)

7. What do you think Frothingham meant by the phrase "providential school of adversity"? In what way did adversity promote the providential purpose of achieving American union? (See *Union*, p. 322)

8. The "common interest" of the colonies necessitated "a common council." William Penn's plan of union for nine colonies embraced such a common council. What was the stated purpose of Penn's Plan? Why did the colonies not like the plan? And why did Great Britain not like it either? (See *Union*, p. 323)

9. As the colonies moved slowly, but steadily, toward continental union, a national spirit slowly developed. Read the definition of an American in *The Letters from an American Farmer*, on p. 319 of *Union*. Then write your own answer to the question: Who is an American?

10. As pressures upon the liberties of all Americans increased, John Adams wrote: "No one of any feelings, born and educated in this happy country, can consider the usurpations that are mediating for all our countrymen and all their posterity without the utmost agonies of heart and many tears."

Consider carefully Adams' eloquent advice on p. 320 of your text. Are the objections he outlines as necessary for the defense of American liberty as important to us today as they were in his time? If so, summarize what you believe should be the role of the people, the pulpit, the bar, and the colleges today in defense of American liberty.

STEP FOUR:

FURTHER STUDY OF PRINCIPLES AND LEADING IDEAS

Study *The Acts of Tyranny of Great Britain from 1660–1765* in your text on pp. 339–343, and see also pp. 399–400 on the accumulated burden of these acts of tyranny.

Recollect that for a long time the colonies acknowledged the right of Great Britain to govern their trade but that, as time went on, they found increasingly galling its prohibition against trading to their advantage with nations other than Great Britain. But particularly offensive were the prohibitions on colonial manufacture of goods for the colonists' own use and inter-colonial sale of these goods. (See the Woolen Act of 1699 and the Hat Act of 1732, *Union*, p. 341)

Write an Essay on *The Accumulated Burden of British Acts of Tyranny* from Charles II's Navigation Act of 1660 to the Stamp Act of 1765.

(*Note*: The Stamp Act was a tax on all printed paper used in business transactions. It greatly increased the cost of doing business. "By this act, a ream of bail bonds, stamped, cost f100; a ream of common printed ones before had been sold for f15. A ream of stamped policies of insurance cost f190; a ream of common ones without stamps, f20. Other papers were taxed in the same proportion." See *Old South Leaflet No. 156*, p. 112)

In your essay, discuss the many different items of colonial manufacture that were affected by these Acts of Tyranny. Take up the following questions that affect Americans today: 1) Is political liberty alone sufficient to keep a people free and independent or must they also have economic liberty? 2) What will it avail a people to have the right to elect representatives to their state legislatures to make the laws, if these representatives shackle commerce and industry with unjust and/or excessive taxation on productivity? (If you wish, consult *Christian History*, Vol. I, p. 292, for some thought-provoking material to help you answer these questions)

STEP FIVE:

ORIGINAL THOUGHT

Read the material on the Albany Plan in your text on pp. 325–338. Consider that it was the Crown that proposed a convention be held in Albany in 1694 to form a defensive union of the colonies and that the royal governors were quick to support the suggestion. Consequently, many colonists looked upon the Albany Congress with disfavor. But what came out of this meeting was extremely important to the history of the development of American union.

Historian John Fiske says that it was the prospect of immediate war with the French that led to the call for a congress of all the colonies. In the minds of most of the delegates to this Congress, Fiske says, "the primary purpose of the meeting was to make sure of the friendship of the Six Nations [of the Iroquois] and to organize a general scheme of operations against the French. The secondary purpose was to prepare some plan of confederation which all the colonies might be persuaded to adopt. New Hampshire, Massachusetts, Rhode Island, Connecticut, New York, Pennsylvania, and Maryland — only seven colonies of the thirteen — sent commissioners to this congress. The people showed little interest in the movement. It does not appear that any public meetings were held in favour of it. Among the newspapers, the only one which warmly approved of it seems to have been the 'Pennsylvania Gazette,' edited by Benjamin Franklin, which appeared with a union device and the motto 'Unite or Die!'" (John Fiske, *The American Revolution*, Boston & New York, 1898, Vol. I, p. 7)

But to Benjamin Franklin who drafted the Albany Plan, the most important purpose was colonial union. Without such a union among themselves, there could be no unity of purpose with the Six Nations.

"The circumstances of Franklin's life, no less than the vast sweep of his intelligence, had fitted him for sounder and wider views of the political needs of the time than were taken by most of his contemporaries.... It was to Franklin that the [Albany] plan was chiefly due...." (*Ibid.*)

A PROPOSAL FOR A SELF-SUSTAINING FEDERAL GOVERNMENT

Fiske also observed that it was "to the credit of its great author, that this scheme... contemplated *the formation of a self-sustaining federal government and not of a mere league*." (*Ibid.*, p. 9) Fiske also quotes historian Richard Frothingham on the Albany Plan:

"It designed to confer on the representatives of the people the power of making laws acting directly on individuals, and appointing officers to execute them, and yet not to interfere with the execution of the laws operating on the same individuals by the local officers."

A Valuable Precedent for the Federal Constitution

This was why it was, as Fiske notes, "much more complete than the scheme of confederation agreed on in Congress in 1777, and it afforded a valuable precedent for the much more elaborate and perfect Federal Constitution of 1787." (*Ibid.*)

Consider also the explanation of the Plan given in *Union*, pp. 332-333, of the providential role of Benjamin Franklin at the Albany Congress and later at the Federal Convention in the search for "a more perfect union."

Write an essay on *Providential Steps Toward American Union* with special emphasis on the Albany Plan taking into consideration the material in your text on pp. 337–338 dealing with the providential development of American union.

A Few Words About Benjamin Franklin and Deism

To many Christians today, who have been taught that Franklin was a deist, it seems shocking to think of him as being used of Providence for such constructive purposes. But the fact is that Franklin really does not fit into the deist category.

Deism has been defined as a belief that "God has no immediate relation with the world... the 'absentee landlord' view" and "that the traditional God need hardly be appealed to since man finds in nature the necessary guides for moral and religious living." (Vergilius Ferm in Dagobert D. Runes, *Dictionary of Philosophy*, 1960, cited in Rousas John Rushdoony, *This Independent Republic*, 1978, p. 5)

Franklin does not appear to have shared these views. He seems to have been a close student of the Bible, and his writings reflect a devout faith in Divine Providence. In a memorable speech at the Constitutional Convention, he remarked that during the Revolutionary War, "all of us who were engaged in the struggle must have observed frequent instances of a superintending Providence in our Favor" and that it was "to that kind Providence we owe this happy opportunity of consulting in peace on the means of establishing our future felicity." He also declared that "without His concurring aid we shall succeed in this political building no better than the builders of Babel; we shall be divided by our partial little local interests; our projects will be confounded and we ourselves shall become a byword down the future ages." (See Isaac Cornelison, *The Relation of Religion to Civil Government in the United States of America: A State without a Church, but not Without a Religion*, 1895, for a full text of this eloquent speech)

These are certainly not the words of a deist. Indeed, in his *Autobiography*, he tells of his rejection of deism as a young man after becoming (briefly) "a thorough Deist." But the unjust conduct of some of his deist friends towards him and his own poor conduct toward others soon persuaded him that deism was a poor system to follow. (See Benjamin Franklin, *The Autobiography and Other Writings*, with commentary by Frank Donovan, 1963, pp. 64–65)

This is not to say that Franklin was a Christian. He still had doubts concerning the deity of Jesus Christ which he expressed in a letter to his friend, the Rev. Ezra Stiles, President of Yale, a few weeks before his death. Whether his doubts were finally resolved, no one can be certain, but what is certain is that Franklin was deeply influenced by the Christian view of life which he had imbibed from devout parents. He was also influenced by his many Christian friends, such as the evangelist, George Whitefield, who prayed for his conversion.

Step Six:

What Christian Principles and Ideas Identify the American Political Union?

1. The first attempt at American union embodied the theocratic principle. "The first conception of an American Union entertained by the founders of New England was to join in political bonds only those colonies in which the people were of a similar way of thinking in theology, when, in the spirit of a theocracy, they aimed to form a Christian State in the bosom of the Church. This was embodied in the New England Confederacy (1643 to 1684)." (See *Union*, p. 304)

2. Experience in fighting the French and Indian wars served as a providential school of adversity to bring home to the colonies the need for union. (*Union*, p. 322)

3. William Penn's Plan of Union (1698) was distinctly American in that it "recognized colonial customs, and is marked by the spirit of fraternity and patriotism, and by that aim in the common good which characterized the career of William Penn." (p. 323)

4. The spirit and aims of American union, as supported by "the popular party" in America were very different from those of the "party of the

prerogative." It aimed at a *voluntary union* based on local self-government and a free trade system, whereas the prerogative party favored a *compulsory union* of the colonies by Act of Parliament and preservation of the monarchical system of British trade monopoly in the colonies. (pp. 324–325)

5. The Albany Plan of Benjamin Franklin was a great step forward in the development of American federal theory. (See p. 49 of this lesson) "The Albany Plan was designed to establish for all Americans one government, based on the consent of the governed, and limited to general purposes, while it left to the local governments their separate functions." (*Union,* p. 332)

6. But before this grand vision of union could take shape, six important developments had to take place: 1) the growth of public opinion in favor of union; 2) the rise of a sentiment of nationality; 3) the actual possession of sovereignty; 4) long training of the people to think politically; 5) leadership representative of the fundamental political principles of the people; and 6) the growth of a fraternal sentiment between the people of all the colonies. (See *Union,* p. 333)

LESSON EIGHT

THE COLONISTS UNITE TO DEFEND THEIR LIBERTY

So speak ye, and so do,
as they that shall be judged by the law of liberty.
(James 2:12)

With this lesson, you are now entering the decade of debate with Great Britain (1765–1775). Beginning with the Stamp Act of 1765, the colonists vigorously defended their liberty under the laws of God and the English Constitution. Many well-reasoned arguments were published in newspapers or in pamphlet form, and as "Instructions" to colonial legislators, and petitions or remonstrances to the king and parliament.

THE LEADERSHIP OF THE CLERGY

The colonial clergy played a significant role during this great debate. Ministers pointed out repeatedly in their sermons the close connection between civil and religious liberty. They often reminded their congregations that there was no example in history of a people retaining their religious liberty once their civil liberty was lost. They elevated the tone of the debate by reminding the people that the blessings of civil liberty flowed from Christ's Law of Liberty.

By 1773, we find Rev. Simeon Howard preaching an Artillery-Election Sermon on Galations 5:1, "Stand fast therefore in the liberty wherewith Christ hath made us free," in which he declared that although these words originally referred "to that freedom from the Jewish law which the gospel confers on the church of God; yet the reason of the inference holds good in the case of any other real and valuable liberty which men have a right to. . . ." (See *Consider*

and Ponder, p. 193) Pointing out that "the destruction of civil liberty is generally fatal to *religion*," *he remarks that "The latter has seldom existed long in any place without the former." It was a duty of men "to defend that liberty, with which providence has made them free." (Ibid.*, p. 203)

In 1775, at the close of this ten-year period of intense debate, Rev. John Zubly preached a sermon on The Law of Liberty in Savannah, Georgia on the text from James 2:12, "So speak ye, and so do, as they that shall be judged by the Law of Liberty." This pastor pointed out that the law of liberty, of which the Apostle wrote, not only liberates man from the bondage of sin and death, but "bears also the most friendly aspect to the liberty of man" (p. 515) and, indeed, that "liberty has taken its seat only in Christendom, and that the highest degree of freedom is pleaded for and enjoyed by such as make profession of the gospel." (p. 518)

Rev. Zubly also declared that "The Christian religion . . . no where requires a blind and unlimited obedience on the part of the subjects; nor does it vest any absolute and arbitrary power in the rulers. It is an institution for the benefit, and not for the distress, of mankind." He insists that, "The gospel gives no higher authority to magistrates than to be '*the ministers of God, for the good of the subject.' Rom. xiii.*

Rev. Zubly repreatedly made the point in his sermon that there can be no liberty without law, for "as

53

laws which take away the natural rights of men, are unjust and oppressive, so all liberty which is not regulated by law, is a delusive phantom, and unworthy of the glorious name." (p. 515) He concluded his sermon by warning of "the extreme absurdity of struggling for civil liberty, and yet to continue slaves to sin and lust" urging all to become "the willing servants of the Lord JESUS CHRIST," because "where the spirit of the Lord is, there is liberty; and 'if the Son makes you free,' THEN, and not till then, 'SHALL YOU BE FREE INDEED.'" (P. 522)

By such sermons as these, the clergy prepared the people and their leaders to make an intelligent defense of their God-bestowed liberty and Christian self-government. (There is more on the influence of the clergy during this crucial 10-year period of debate with Great Britain in the following lesson.)

LEADERS IN THE CIVIL SPHERE EMERGE

Afflictive as it was, the Stamp Tax, levied on the colonists in 1765 without their consent, provided an impetus toward colonial union. The increasing adversity the colonists experienced in their relation with the Mother Country served providentially to extend and deepen this sentiment and to accelerate development of practical means to effect union.

Prominent citizens emerged as leaders of a movement to defend American liberties. Among them was Boston lawyer, James Otis, whose paper, *The Rights of the Colonies Asserted and Proved* was one of the most influential papers produced at the outset of the quarrel over the Stamp Act. Another Massachusetts leader was Samuel Adams who drafted the *Boston Instructions* to the Massachusetts Legislature, another masterly statement of colonial rights and liberties at the time of the Stamp Act crisis.

NO TAXATION WITHOUT REPRESENTATION

Now, was first heard the subsequently famous phrase, "no taxation without representation." Taxing them without their consent was, the colonists firmly believed, an exercise of power without right. Therefore, they looked upon the Stamp Act as invalid.

STEP ONE:
PRINCIPLES TO PONDER

1. PARLIAMENT'S TAXATION OF THE COLONIES VIOLATES THE GENERAL PRINCIPLES OF LIBERTY

"It was generally acknowledged that the parent country might exercise a sovereign dominion over the whole empire, and that while it was guarded by contract, and exercised for the general emolument, it was safe and might not be resisted.... But the right of taxing the colonies without their consent, was universally reprobated, as inconsistent with their natural charter, and constitutional rights. Ancient usage was pleaded against it as well as the general principles of liberty." (Rev. Jedediah Morse, *Union,* p. 351)

2. PARLIAMENTS ARE ANSWERABLE TO A HIGHER AUTHORITY

"Parliaments are in all cases to declare what is for the good of the whole; but it is not the DECLARATION of parliament that makes it so; There must be in every instance, a higher authority, viz. GOD." (James Otis, *Union,* p. 369)

3. LEGISLATURES ARE BOUND BY THE FIRST PRINCIPLES OF LAW AND JUSTICE

"These are their bounds [of the legislative], which by God and nature are fixed, hitherto have they a right to come, and no further.

"'1. To govern by stated laws. 2. Those laws should have no other end ultimately, but the good of the people. 3. Taxes are not to be laid on the people, but by their consent in person, or by deputation. 4. Their whole power is not transferable.' (See Locke on Government. B. 11. C. 11.)

"These are the first principles of law and justice, and the great barriers of a free state, and of the British constitution in particular." (James Otis, Union, p. 387)

STEP TWO:
READING FOR LEADING IDEAS

Read pp. 353–360 in your text on "The Art of Taxing," and pp. 361–367 on "Town, Province and Assembly Assert Their Rights."

As you read, notice that although England had left the colonies to tax themselves for a century and a half, this situation suddenly changed in 1763 as England's Chancellor of the Exchequer, George Grenville, along with other English politicians, conceived the idea of an internal tax on the colonists. It was to be levied ostensibly to support a military establishment in America of some 20 regiments. It was said in Great Britain that the colonists had never paid for the English regiments that had defended them in the wars in which England had been engaged and which the colonists had also become involved. But was this the full story?

THE COLONISTS LOOK TO THEMSELVES FOR THEIR DEFENSE

You will recollect that, although the colonists "asked that English troops might be sent over by the government to meet French troops," they were left to their own resources for many years. The taxes they had to levy on themselves for defense against the French and their Indian allies had "pressed heavily on industry." (See *Union*, p. 322)

Lord Brougham later admitted: "The whole expense of civil government in the British North American colonies, previous to the Revolution, did not amount to eighty thousand pounds sterling, which was paid by the produce of their taxes. The military establishments, the garrisons and the forts in the old colonies, cost the mother-country nothing." (*Union*, p. 332)

THE COLONIES: A SOURCE OF WEALTH TO THE MOTHER COUNTRY

Consider, too, that Great Britain's American colonies had been a source of great wealth and prosperity to the Mother Country. Rev. Jedidiah Morse writes that "the settlement and protection of the colonies was not at the expense of Great Britain, so it is equally evident, that this increase of their trade was not at the expense or diminution of the general trade of the kingdom, for this increased during the same period from six, to sixteen millions." (See *Union*, p. 352)

FUNDING ENGLAND'S NATIONAL DEBT WITH TAXES FROM AMERICA

The real reason for the desire for increased revenue from America was the staggering national debt under which England was laboring at the time. It amounted to "the enormous sum of a hundred and forty-eight millions," and because Englishmen "already groaned under the grievous load of taxes" levied to meet this debt, the British ministry conceived of a plan "for easing the inhabitants of Great Britain" by raising revenue from the American colonies through parliamentary taxation. (See *Union*, p. 353)

Grenville was determined to impose some kind of internal taxation on the colonists and did not greatly care what form it took. "If the stamp duty is disliked, I am willing to change it for any other equally productive. If you object to the Americans being taxed by Parliament, save yourself the trouble of the discussion, for I am determined on the measure." (*Union*, p. 360)

It shocked the colonists to learn that "not a single member of either house [of parliament] doubted the right of parliament to impose a stamp duty or any other tax upon them" and to learn also that the King had heartily approved of Grenville's plan.

ENSURING THE DEPENDENCE OF THE COLONIES ON GREAT BRITAIN

It was Great Britain's plan to ensure the dependence of her American colonies on the Mother Country by a variety of means: by internal taxation, by remodeling of the colonial governments, and by renewed and strict enforcement of the navigation acts. But, note the far-sighted words of Richard Henry Lee of Virginia when he heard the news of the passage of the Stamp Act: "The ways of Heaven are inscrutable," he wrote to a friend, "this step of the mother country, though intended to secure our dependence, may produce a fatal resentment and be subversive of that end." (p. 360)

METHODS OF RESISTANCE TO BRITISH TYRANNY

One of the first methods of resistance to parliamentary tyranny chosen by the Massachusetts patriots began at the local level in the *Instructions,* penned by Samuel Adams, which Boston sent to its representatives in the Massachusetts assembly. (See *Union*, pp. 361–364)

Another constructive method of resistance they chose was to instruct their London Agent to plead their cause in the English capital explaining to their British cousins why they objected to the Act. (See letter to Jasper Maudit drafted by James Otis, in your text, pp. 366–367)

Note, too, that the Massachusetts assembly (known as the General Court) appointed a committee "to acquaint the other [colonial] governments with these instructions and in the name and behalf of the House to 'desire the several assemblies on this continent to join with them in the same measures.'" (*Union*, p. 365) This appeal to the other colonies was to have far-reaching results.

STEP THREE:

QUESTIONS FOR INVENTION

1. In addition to the Stamp Act, what other measures did Great Britain take in 1764 to increase revenue from America? (See *Union*, pp. 342, 356)

2. Who was the first man to sound the alarm regarding the Stamp Tax in Boston in May 1764? (See *Union*, p. 364)

3. What important motion did Samuel Adams make at the Boston Town Meeting called to discuss the Stamp Act? What role did he play in helping the town of Boston to form "the cornerstone of its policy" regarding this act? (*Ibid.*)

4. In the *Boston Instructions*, where do we see the New England philosophy of government and the relations of the people to their representatives? Is their freedom on both sides? What freedom do the representatives have and what freedom do the people reserve for themselves? (See *Union*, p. 362)

5. What do the *Boston Instructions* outline as their main expectations from their representatives in regard to the Stamp Act? (*Ibid.*)

6. What other taxes did the *Boston Instructions* foresee might soon follow the Stamp Tax? (*Union*, p. 364)

7. At what rights do such taxes strike? (*Ibid.*)

8. Do you think that Samuel Adams exaggerated the case when he said that if taxes were laid on the colonists without their consent they would be reduced from the status of "free subjects" to that of "tributary slaves"? Or is this a fair description of the inevitable outcome when a people have no control over taxation? Explain.

9. In the Massachusetts legislature's letter to their London agent, what is the doctrine that James Otis defines "as agreeable to the law of nature and nations and to the divine dictates of natural and revealed religion?" (p. 366)

10. The Stamp Act threatened great financial hardship to the colonies but, according to James Otis, it had one good effect. Explain what that effect was. (See *Union*, p. 368)

STEP FOUR:

FURTHER STUDY OF PRINCIPLES AND LEADING IDEAS

The Rights of the British Colonies Asserted and Proved by James Otis is a paper well worth studying in some detail in order to discover the views that many colonists shared at this time of increasing tensions in their relationship with Great Britain. As you have already learned in his discussion of the Law of Nations (Lesson Six, Step Five), Otis did more than discuss the rights of the colonies under the English Constitution.

TRACING GOVERNEMT TO ITS SOURCE AND ORIGIN

Otis traced government to its source and origin in the laws of God. In his review of mankind's various opinions on the origin of civil government, he rejects the idea that it is founded in grace, by which he is referring to the Divine Right of Kings theory or the rule of the Bishops of Rome or the claim of Roman Pontiffs to absolute rule by appointment from God. Nor does he believe that government springs *merely* from compact or the need to protect property.

"What shall we say then? Is not government founded on grace? No. Nor or force? No. Nor on compact? Nor property? Not altogether on either. Has it any solid foundation? any chief corner stone, but what accident, chance or confusion may lay one moment and destroy the next? I think it has an everlasting foundation in the unchangeable will of GOD, the author of nature, whose laws never vary. . . .

"Government is therefore most evidently founded on the necessities of our nature. It is by no means an arbitrary thing, depending merely on compact or human will for its existence." (*Union*, p. 373)

THE END OR PURPOSE OF GOVERNMENT

Note particularly what Otis had to say on the end or purpose of government (on pp. 374–375 of your text) and the only power that can be strictly called supreme and absolute. Why did he believe that supreme, unlimited power in the hands of one person goes counter to "the first principles of reason"? If one man should not have the supreme power, who should have it and how should that power be exercised in order to accord with the divine will? (See pp. 374–377 of your text)

GOVERNMENT AS TRUST

In citing John Locke, Otis made the important point that the legislative body of a commonwealth should be supreme, but only insofar as it fulfills the terms of its trust which are determined by the people whom it represents. "For all power given, with trust for attaining an end, being limited by that end, whenever that end is manifestly neglected, or opposed, the trust must necessarily be forfeited."

(Note that already — in 1764 — Otis cites Locke on the grounds for overthrowing an unjust government. See p. 380)

THE NATURAL RIGHTS OF ALL MEN VINDICATED

You have already studied the section of Otis' paper on the relations between colonies and the Mother Country as taught by Grotius and Puffendorf and the natural rights of the colonists. Now, notice that Otis did not limit the enjoyment of these rights to the white man, but that he also included the black man. (See p. 383) Note what he has to say about the slave trade.

PARLIAMENT IS BOUND BY THE CONSTITUTION

Otis also posed a very provocative question when he asked what would happen to the rights of the colonies if Parliament suddenly annihilated all their charters? Would they thus lose all their rights, both civil and religious, with one stroke of the pen? Did Parliament have the *right* to strip the colonists of their liberties under the English constitution? Otis declared that Parliament could not legally do so, because there was nothing in the laws of England giving Parliament such a right.

As he explained further on, "The parliament cannot make 2 and 2, 5: Omnipotency cannot do it. The supreme power in a state, is *jus dicere* [to state the law] only: — *jus dare* [to make the law], strictly speaking, belongs alone to God." (See the conclusion of his line of reasoning in the last paragraph on p. 388)

THE IMPORTANCE OF FIRST PRINCIPLES

Throughout *The Rights of the Colonies,* Otis referred often to "first principles" which, as we have seen, was characteristic of the Founding Fathers. They always sought to trace all things back to these first principles, and this was in harmony with their conviction that God is a God of order who has created the principles by which he governs all things. See particularly Otis' citation of six "first principles of law and justice" as stated by John Locke (on pp. 386–387 of your text).

Otis gives the reader a concise summary of his paper on p. 391. The abdication he refers to here is the one forced on James II, and the revolution to which he refers is "the Glorious Revolution" of 1688 which placed James II's daughter, Mary, and her husband, William of Orange, on the English throne as constitutional monarchs.

After you finish reading this paper, write your own summary of the leading ideas Otis developed.

Can you relate these ideas to our own government today? For example:

- Is it not still true that, under our Constitutional form of government, Congress may not make whatever laws it pleases, but only those that conform to the Constitution?

- Is it not also still true that the Chief Executive cannot legally make Executive Orders violative of the Constitution? Is it not true, that the Chief Executive is not to *make* law, but only to see that the laws of the land are carried out properly?

- Is it not true that the Supreme Court has no legal right to interpret the laws in a way that violates the *intentions* of the writers of the Constitution and the people who ratified it?

Consider, too, the *binding nature* of the *Higher Law* to which our Founding Fathers believed all human constitutions and statutes should conform.

STEP FIVE:
ORIGINAL THOUGHT

Between 1765–1775, Samuel Adams became one of the foremost leaders in America. He was among the first to oppose the new Stamp Act. Long known as "the father of the Revolution," his efforts have in recent times been disparaged and misrepresented. "But," as Rosalie J. Slater reminds us, "the shining lights of the past cannot be extinguished when, once again, we examine our history with the light of Christianity." (*T & L,* p. 251) Although Samuel Adams has often been categorized by modern authors as a political propagandist and rabble rouser, this was far from the case. As earlier historians well knew, his was a sterling Christian character and his political insights were clear and true. (Note what George Bancroft wrote concerning his character on p. 361 of your text.)

THE CHRISTIAN UPBRINGING
OF SAMUEL ADAMS

William V. Wells, in his *Life and Public Services of Samuel Adams,* makes this observation on his Christian upbringing:

"The mother of Samuel Adams . . . early imbued her children with reverence for the Christian virtues which she practised. To the scrupulous attention of his parents to devotional subjects must have been greatly due the religious turn of mind which was a prevailing trait throughout the life of the son." (*T & L*, p. 255)

A CONSISTENT CHRISTIAN CHARACTER

Miss Slater discusses the "consistent Christian character" of Samuel Adams, which was seen in the simplicity and frugality of his household and in his "devotion to the principles of Christian liberty" and his "absolutely selfless devotion to the service of his country."

"This was expressed," she writes, "in the *tireless activity* of his efforts to write, to debate, *to encourage the understanding and practice of self-government at the local level of each individual community and each individual colony*. Samuel Adams was a hard worker. He never sought a political office for personal benefit but served from the early years simply as *a man of integrity and conviction* and willingness to sacrifice all — if need be, for the principles of justice and liberty. His standards of Christian morality as qualification for political office were exemplified in his own *devotion to Christ and country* and the *consistency of his conduct in everything he undertook*." (*T & L*, p. 255, emphasis added)

Samuel Adams' unswerving perseverance in the cause of Christian liberty and self-government was indeed an example of the Apostle Paul's injunction to the Galatians: "And let us not be weary in well-doing: for in due season we shall reap, if we faint not." (Galatians 6:9)

EDUCATING HIS FELLOW COLONISTS IN CHRISTIAN SELF-GOVERNMENT WITH UNION

Along with his patient efforts to educate his fellow colonists in Massachusetts in the importance of maintaining their local self-government were his equally patient efforts to bring together all of the colonies in a grand continental union in defense of their God-given rights.

In working to achieve his political ends, his manners were quiet and conciliatory and he worked well with men of all backgrounds within his own colony and with the patriots who emerged in the other colonies during the ten-year period of constitutional debate between 1765–1775.

Thomas Jefferson said that "Samuel Adams was constantly holding caucuses of distinguished men, in which the measures to be pursued were generally determined upon.... He ascribed great influence to Samuel Adams in promoting the Revolution." (See *Christian History*, p. 351)

His great paper, *The Rights of the Colonists as Men, as Christians, and as Subjects* (1772), has been called "the most systematic presentation of the American cause." (See *Christian History*, Vol. I, pp. 365–370 for excerpts)

VIRTUE AND KNOWLEDGE: THE PEOPLE'S GREAT SECURITY

Samuel Adams was one of the first to realize that the colonies must claim their independence from the Mother Country. But he knew that the people must have Christian virtue if they were to found their new nation on a solid footing.

His Christian political wisdom is seen in this far-sighted warning: "A general Dissolution of Principles and Manners will more surely overthrow the Liberties of America than the whole Force of the Common Enemy. While the People are virtuous they cannot be subdued; but when once they lose their Virtue they will be ready to surrender their Liberties to the first external or internal Invader.... If Virtue and Knowledge are diffused among the People, they will never be enslaved. This will be their great Security." (*T & L*, p. 251)

Samuel Adams understood, therefore, the need of educating children in the Christian principles of government, as is seen by this eloquent passage from his writings:

"Let divines and philosophers, statesmen and patriots, unite their endeavors to renovate the age, by impressing the minds of men with the importance of educating their little boys and girls, of inculcating in the minds of youth the fear and love of the Deity and universal philanthropy, and, in subordination to these great principles, the love of their country; *of instructing them in the art of self-government, without which they never can act a wise part in the government of societies, great or small; in short, of leading them in the study and practice of the exalted virtues of the Christian system....*" (See *Christian History*, Vol. I, p. XIV, emphasis added)

EDUCATION IN SOUND POLITICAL PRINCIPLES

Samuel Adams not only saw the need for independence and promoted it unceasingly, but he also saw that in order to become an independent people, Americans needed to be educated in sound political principles. "He knew," says Rosalie J. Slater, "that, in the tradition of freemen, they must *discuss, dispute,* and *debate* the implication of their position. It ws largely through his tireless efforts that Adams brought into being the *Committees of Correspondence* and kept them functioning through the years prior to the revolution. It was particularly through his own vigorous participation in the Boston Town Meeting that he encouraged public discussion as well as private correspondence as a means of self-education." (*T & L,* p. 254) (*Note:* You will be studying more about Samuel Adams and the development of the Committees of Correspondence in Lesson 11)

Write a brief paper on Adams discussing the special traits of Christian character he possessed which eminently qualified him for political leadership. Note what a force Adams was in the development of *both* local self-government and union. (For additional material on Adams, read *T & L,* pp. 251–257)

Step Six:

What Christian Principles and Ideas Identify the American Political Union?

1. During the 10-year decade of debate with the Mother Country, the colonists began to claim their rights not only under the English Constitution but also under God's laws revealed in Scripture and in His Law of Nature. (See James Otis, *The Rights of the British Colonies,* pp. 370–391)

2. In 1764, the colonists were still proud of their relation to the Mother Country. They revered the English Constitution as the best in the world and as belonging to them as much as it did to their British cousins. But, in asserting their right to local self-government, the colonists introduced a new idea of union—the germ of American federalism—which was alien to the aims of Great Britain to establish a centralized government in the colonies directed by Parliament and the King's ministers. (See *Union,* pp. 352–353)

3. In their resistance to the Stamp Tax, the colonists put forth the theory known as "no taxation without representation," *i.e.,* the colonists believed they could not be constitutionally taxed except by themselves through their own representatives in their own colonial assemblies. This was a challenge to the power of the English Parliament—in which they had no representation—over the colonies. It was stated that the power of parliament was circumscribed within constitutional bounds and that to exceed these bounds was to exercise power without right. (See *Union,* p. 365)

4. It was a time when the colonists in Boston gathered under the Liberty Tree and declared "Liberty, Property and No Stamps!" Now was heard the words which were to become the motto of the War of Independence: "Life, liberty and property!" In the *Boston Instructions,* Samuel Adams warned of the dangers to property inherent in Great Britain's asserted right to tax them without their consent: "For if our trade may be taxed, why not our lands? Why not the produce of our lands, and every thing we possess or make use of? This we apprehend annihilates our charter right to govern and tax ourselves.... If taxes are laid upon us in any shape without our having a legal representation where they are laid, are we not reduc'd from the character of free subjects to the miserable state of tributary slaves?" (See *Christian History,* Vol. I, p. 300, and *Union,* p. 364)

LESSON NINE

AMERICANS ACT
IN UNION

For rulers are not a terror to good works, but to the evil.
Wilt thou not be afraid of the power?
Do that which is good, and thou shalt have praise of the same:
for he is the minister of God to thee for good.
(Romans 13:3–4)

In this lesson, you will learn that the colonists not only objected to the new Stamp Tax and the renewed trade duties also imposed by Great Britain at this time; they also objected to *their mode of enforcement*. A colonist accused of failing to pay the Stamp Tax or the trade duties would not be tried by *a jury of his peers* according to the English Constitution. Instead, he would be tried by British naval and military officers, and his case would be decided by *a single judge*. (See *Union*, p. 400)

THE CLERGY LEAD THE PEOPLE TO RESIST ENCROACHMENT ON THEIR GOD-GIVEN RIGHTS

As you have learned in Lesson Eight, the clergy led the people to resist these encroachments by the king and parliament upon their rights. Jonathan Mayhew, a prominent Boston minister and friend of patriot leaders, James Otis and Samuel Adams, declared:

"The king is as much bound by his oath not to infringe the legal rights of the people, as the people are bound to yield subjection to him. From whence it follows that as soon as the prince sets himself above the law, he loses the king in the tyrant. He does, to all intents and purposes, un-king himself by acting out of and beyond that sphere which the [English] constitution allows him to move in, and in such cases

he has no more right to be obeyed than any inferior officer who acts beyond his commission. The subject's obligation to allegiance then ceases, of course, and to resist him is not more rebellion than to resist any foreign invader... it is making use of the means, and the only means, which God has put into their power for mutual and self-defense." (cited by Peter Marshall and David Manuel, *The Light and the Glory,* 1977, pp. 264–265)

That a people may lawfully resist those who set themselves above the law (even a king) is reiterated in many of the Election and Artillery Sermons of the Colonial period. See, for example, Simeon Howard's Artillery-Election Sermon (1773) and Rev. David Jones' Continental Fast Day Sermon (1775) in *C & P* on pp. 193–205 and 536–542, respectively.

One of the most important sermons at the time of the Stamp Act was Rev. Stephen Johnson's Fast Day Sermon which dealt with the enslaving character of the Stamp Tax. (See Step Four of this lesson) To scholar Bernard Bailyn, this sermon was a prototype of many more written in the same vein during the ensuing 10 years.

LAY LEADERS INSPIRED BY THEIR MINISTERS

Providentially, as you have learned, important colonial laymen like James Otis and Samuel Adams of Massachusetts began to play a prominent role on the political scene. In this lesson, you will meet Patrick Henry, who came to the fore at the time of the Stamp Act and who mobilized the resistance to it in Virginia.

The political leaders in both Massachusetts and Virginia were inspired by their ministers to pursue a policy of *constructive opposition* to British measures.

THE STAMP ACT CONGRESS AND POLITICAL RESISTANCE TO THE STAMP TAX

At the Stamp Act Congress, the delegates from nine colonies, stated their position in a declaration of rights and grievances, and proceeded to explain their case to Great Britain in more detail by means of *petition* to the King and the House of Commons and a *memorial* to the House of Lords.

THE COLONIES ALSO UNITE IN ECONOMIC RESISTANCE

In addition to these *political methods* of resistance to the Stamp Tax, which educated their fellow colonists in English constitutional history and reminded Great Britain of their rights under the English Constitution, the colonies, led by New York, also employed the *economic method* of resistance. Shortly after the Stamp Act Congress, they began to enter into agreements not to import any more goods from England until their grievances were redressed.

RESISTANCE RESTING ON BIBLICAL PRINCIPLES OF GOVERNMENT

Whether political or economic resistance, the colonists rested it upon the Biblical principles of government the clergy had taught them. "Was the Bible quoted as demanding deference to all in authority? 'This,' it was insisted, 'is to add dulness to impiety: 'for tyranny is no government....'

"'Power is a sad thing,' wrote the Presbyterians of Philadelphia: 'Our mother should remember we are children, and not slaves.' 'When all Israel saw that the king harkened not unto them,' responded the Calvinists of the North, 'the people answered the king, saying: 'What portion have we in David? What inheritance in the son of Jesse? To your tents, O Israel!' ... 'I would bear allegiance to King George,' said one who called himself a lover of Truth, 'but not be a slave to his British subjects....'

"Thus opinion was echoed from mind to mind, as the sun's rays beam from many clouds, all differing in tints, but every one taking its hue from the same fire.... Hope began to rise that American rights and liberties might safely be trusted 'to the watchfulness

of a united continent....'" (George Bancroft, *Union,* p. 415)

STEP ONE: PRINCIPLES TO PONDER

1. THE GOSPEL AND LIBERTY

"The Gospel promises liberty and permits resistance." (Rev. Jonathan Mayhew, *Union,* p. 412)

2. A FUNDAMENTAL PRINCIPLE OF THE PATRIOTS WAS: THAT LEGISLATORS WHO TAKE AWAY THE PROPERTY OF THE PEOPLE OR GOVERN THEM ARBITRARILY CREATE A STATE OF WAR

"Whenever the Legislators endeavour to take away, and destroy the property of the People, or to reduce them to Slavery under arbitrary Power, they put themselves into a state of War with the People, who are thereupon absolved from any farther Obedience, and are left to the common Refuge, which God hath provided for all Men, against force and Violence." (John Locke, *Union,* p. 410)

3. MAN HAS CERTAIN GOD-GIVEN RIGHTS

"You have rights antecedent to all earthly government; rights that cannot be repealed or restrained by human laws; rights derived from the great Legislator of the universe." (John Adams, *Union,* p. 422)

4. THE VIRGINIA RESOLVES AFFIRM THE RIGHT OF LOCAL SELF-GOVERNMENT

"RESOLVED, that his majesty's liege people, of this, his ancient colony, have enjoyed the right of being thus governed by their own assembly, in the article of taxes and internal police, and that the same have never been forfeited, or yielded up...." (*Union,* p. 404)

5. THE STAMP ACT CONGRESS DECLARES THE COLONISTS ARE ENTITLED TO THE SAME RIGHTS AS SUBJECTS BORN IN ENGLAND

"2d. That his majesty's liege subjects in these colonies are entitled to all the inherent rights and privileges of his natural born subjects within the kingdom of Great Britain.

"3d. That it is inseparably essential to the freedom of a people, and the undoubted rights of Englishmen, that no taxes should be imposed on them, but with their own consent, given personally, or by their representatives." (*Union*, pp. 423–424)

STEP TWO:
READING FOR LEADING IDEAS

Virginia's House of Burgess was the only colonial legislative body in session at the time the news reached the colonies in May 1765 that Parliament had indeed passed the Stamp Act. So it was that "Virginia rang the alarm bell for the continent" through the stirring *Resolves* penned by Patrick Henry, then a new member of the House. Henry was a young lawyer from the Virginia frontier country whose burning oratory kindled the flame of patriotism throughout the colonies after the *Resolves* were printed and widely circulated.

THE CHARACTER OF PATRICK HENRY

Patrick Henry (1736–1799) was known throughout his life as a very religious man, and he remained a devoted son of the Anglican church in which he had been baptized. (His uncle, Patrick, was a Church of England minister). But Patrick early learned to value the religious views of other denominations. For 11 years, his mother, a Presbyterian, took him to hear the Rev. Samuel Davies preach to the non-conformists of Hanover County, Virginia. Davies was renowned as a preacher, and it was from listening to his sermons that young Henry learned much about the art of oratory. As a young lawyer, Patrick Henry defended Baptists from persecution by the authorities in his state.

"I AM NOT A VIRGINIAN BUT AN AMERICAN!"

Later in life, he opposed the firmer union outlined in the new Constitution, fearing it would absorb local self-government and individual liberties. But at the time of the Revolution, Henry was a great force for union. At the first Continental Congress of 1774, Henry urged union in glowing words that spoke of a new allegiance: "Where are now your boundaries? The distinctions between Virginians, Pennsylvanians, New Yorkers, New Englanders are no more. I am not a Virginian, but an American!" (See Catherine Drinker Bowen's *John Adams and the American Revolution*, p. 477)

LIBERTY OR DEATH!

At the Virginia Convention at Richmond in 1775, Henry urged independence in words which American school children used to learn by heart.

"What has there been in the conduct of the British ministry for the last ten years to justify hope? . . . There is no longer room for hope. If we wish to be free, we must fight! . . . An appeal to arms and to the God of Hosts is all that is left us! . . . Is life so dear, or peace so sweet, as to be purchased at the price of chains and slavery? Forbid it, Almighty God! — I know not what course others may take; but as for me, give me liberty, or give me death." (For more of his speech, see *Christian History*, Vol. I, p. 346A)

INDEPENDENCE: A BLESSING OR A CURSE?

To his dying day, Henry was particularly proud of the role his *Virginia Resolves* had played in helping to move the country toward continental union. "After his death, there was found among his papers one sealed, and thus endorsed: 'Enclosed are the resolutions of the Virginia Assembly in 1765, concerning the Stamp Act. Let my executors open this paper.'" (William Wirt, *The Life of Patrick Henry*, p. 74) In the envelope was a copy of the *Resolves* as he had drawn them up in his own handwriting. On the back of the paper Henry had written (in part):

"The written resolutions passed in the house of burgesses in May 1765. . . . After a long and warm contest the resolutions passed by a very small majority, perhaps one or two only. The alarm spread throughout America with astonishing quickness. . . . The great point of resistance to British taxation was universally established in the colonies. This brought on the war, which finally separated the two countries, and gave independence to ours. Whether this will prove a blessing or a curse will depend upon the use our people make of the blessing which a gracious God hath bestowed upon us. If they are wise, they will be great and happy. If they are of a contrary character, they will be miserable. Righteousness alone can exalt them as a nation.

"Reader! Whoever thou art, remember this; and in thy sphere, practise virtue thyself, and encourage it in others. — P. Henry." (Quoted in William Wirt, pp. 75–76)

GOD'S HAND IN OUR HISTORY

When Henry spoke up for liberty and local self-government in 1765, and for union in 1774, and for independence in 1775, were these not instances of God's providential hand in our history? Rev. S. J. Foljambe, in his Annual Election Sermon of 1876, saw God's hand in the men He raised up for those times.

"He who makes the times go over us, has always the men ready to meet them. It was so in the era of the Reformation. . . . So, for the times of Republican progress, — when a new nation is to come to its manhood, and new institutions are to be confirmed and established, — he found an Otis and a Henry, the impassioned and triumphant defenders of popular rights. . . ." (See *Consider and Ponder*, p. 52)

It was James Otis who made the next providentially impelled move toward continental union when, on June 6, 1765, he advised the Massachusetts Assembly to call for a Congress of all the colonies to meet in New York. The Assembly's letter was sent out to the colonial legislatures on June 8, 1765. (See *Union*, p. 407) Note the purpose for the meeting as stated in this letter.

Read pp. 392–396 of your text, "The Assemblies Re-Echo James Otis' Speech," and then pp. 398–411, "Virginia Marshals Resistance — Massachusetts Entreats Union — New York Points to Independence."

STEP THREE:

QUESTIONS FOR INVENTION

1. In addition to giving *Instructions* to their legislatures and writing *articles* for the newspapers or *pamphlets* (like that of James Otis'), what other orderly and constructive methods did the colonists use in their opposition to the Stamp Act? (See *Union*, pp. 392–396)

2. On what did the colonists primarily rely in the Memorials and Petitions they sent to England to plead their cause? (See for example, Virginia's *Memorial* to the House of Lords, *Union*, pp. 395–396)

3. What was the *tone* used in these documents? Was it respectful or belligerent? Explain. (*Ibid.*)

4. At this time, when Great Britain controlled our commerce, could foreign ships enter colonial harbors? (See *Union*, p. 399)

5. What was the reason Great Britain had such stringent regulations against intercolonial trade so that the colonists could not even print their own Bibles? (The only exception to this rule was a Bible printed in German and John Eliot's Indian Bible) (*Ibid.*)

6. What was the result in the colonies of Great Britain's policy on the slave trade? (See *Union*, p. 400)

7. What were some other new duties to be collected along with the Stamp Tax? (*Ibid.*)

8. In addition to his gift of oratory, what character trait did Patrick Henry possess which enabled him to present the *Virginia Resolves* to the House of Burgesses and get them to pass it?

9. When Patrick Henry spoke of American independence being either a blessing or a curse, what did he mean? Explain in your words.

10. What did Patrick Henry mean when he spoke of the importance of making a *wise* use of God's blessings? What kind of wisdom do you think he meant?

STEP FOUR:

FURTHER STUDY OF PRINCIPLES AND LEADING IDEAS

REV. STEPHEN JOHNSON'S ARGUMENTS AGAINST THE STAMP TAX

Among the influential writings of New England pastors during the Stamp Act crisis was a series of newspaper articles by Stephen Johnson, pastor of the Congregational Church in Lyme, Connecticut. In, *The New England Clergy and the American Revolution*, Alice M. Baldwin writes:

"In all the newspaper and pamphlet literature of the time none give more clearly the arguments against Great Britain . . . and none speak more plainly of the threatened independence of the colonies."

Rev. Johnson wrote these articles after reading some papers on the Stamp Act (perhaps the *Virginia Resolves*) which set him to thinking. In them he made four important points:

1. That the colonial charters were compacts which, if violated by one of the parties, freed the other from obligation.

2. That the fundamental constitution of England gave the colonists their rights which were antecedent to all earthly government and were derived from "the great Legislator of the Universe" and

that to lose these rights would bring slavery upon their posterity.

3. That the people must not be lulled into a false sense of security, but must be alert to their dangers and to the need for giving their representatives specific instructions to follow in this crisis.

4. That a union of *all* the colonies was essential.

Dr. Bernard Bailyn, one of America's foremost scholars in the field of American colonial history, comments that Johnson's articles were so thorough that they covered almost all the arguments that were to be raised during the following decade.

JOHNSON'S FAST DAY SERMON

Rev. Johnson also presented these political arguments in his Fast Day Sermon of December 18, 1765 which was later published as a pamphlet. Miss Baldwin terms this sermon "one of the most interesting and most vigorous of all the Revolutionary pamphlets." In it, as Dr. Bailyn points out, Rev. Johnson not only explained motives and counseled action based on historical reasoning, but he grounded the political issue in Biblical principles. He drew many parallels between Israel's bondage in Egypt and the bondage of the colonists to Great Britain.

Taking his text from Acts 7:6, 7 and 34, he began by examining "the general nature and consequences of enslaving measures, pointing out that "the enslaving of a free people, the covenant people of God was a very great iniquity."

"Israel were a free people, when they went down to Egypt; they had a right to freedom afterwards, as they had done nothing to forfeit it; and no man nor nation had a right to take it from them."

SLAVERY BY DEGREES

How then did Israel come to be enslaved? It was, he said, by "gradual encroachments, and usurping their rights little by little, until they are all swallowed up in the all-devouring jaws of tyrannic will."

How was this done?

"It was gradually, with increasing usurpations and oppression. They taxed them with heavy burdens, and made them to serve. They set taskmasters over them, to oppress them.

"Then they increased these burdens by demanding the full quota of bricks but refusing to supply the needed materials. They squeezed them harder and harder. Then one day, came the decree to slay all their male infants 'to lessen their increase.'"

What was the policy behind these measures?

1. "To impoverish them effectually."

2. "To prevent their growth: that they might have neither wealth nor power ever to get out of that wretched bondage."

THE PRETEXT FOR PHAROAH'S POLICY

The pretext for Pharoah's policy, says Rev. Johnson, was the possible independence of Israel; for he tells the Egyptians that the Children of Israel were "more and mightier than we." If there were a war, they might side with Egypt's enemies and so escape from Egypt (Exod. 1:9, 10, 11).

Today, Rev. Johnson adds, the "Royal prerogative is to be stretched and exalted . . . to the enslaving of a nation" by using the divine right of kings theory to take away liberty from the people. Now, in England, a loud cry of "independency" is set up against the colonists as a reason for the measures taken against them.

THE INGRATITUDE OF ENGLAND

Rev. Johnson also spoke of the ingratitude of Egypt which had been saved by Joseph (Exod. 1:8), comparing this with the ingratitude of Great Britain for the services of the colonies to the empire over the years.

But, as he pointed out, the attempt to enslave the Israelites opened the way for their deliverance and produced the very thing Egypt feared: their independence.

For they cried out to God to help them and they received Moses as their lawgiver and their deliverer from Egypt. "So it happened [also] in the case of Rehoboam's oppression of the ten tribes. So also in the oppression of Holland [by Spain], which brought in the revolution and independency of those high and mighty states. And it is possible that sooner or later, it may happen to the British colonies."

In forceful language, Rev. Johnson pointed out that no obedience is due to arbitrary, unconstitutional edicts because "it is a flagrant absurdity to suppose a free constitution [such as that of England] empowers any to decree or execute its own destruction. . . . No obedience is due to them by the law of God. . . . *A slavish non-resistance and passive obedience, cannot comport with the will of God."* (Emphasis added) Why not? Because this would only support "misrule and tyranny."

We may not only resist the invasion of our rights "by robbers, highwaymen, or a foreign power" but also by our own rulers if they betray their trust."

BONDAGE AND DESPAIR WORSE THAN DEATH

Rev. Johnson told his congregation that it was their duty to maintain their God-given rights and transmit them to their posterity. "We must not be traitors to God and ourselves and our country," he said, but we should be willing to risk all knowing "that bondage and despair is worse than death."

THE IMPORTANCE OF FASTING AND PRAYER

Rev. Johnson told his congregation that if they were willing to resist, God would hear their prayers as he had heard the prayers of Israel in Egypt. But it was not enough merely to send petitions to the King. He reminded them that when Esther petitioned the King, Mordecai and all the Jews fasted and prayed to God.

During their sojourn in Egypt the Israelites had forgotten the mighty works of God. "Their oppressions brought them wisely and affectionately to consider their relation to God, as his professing, covenant people, and their duties and hopes resulting from hence." So also had the English colonists forgotten Him after the Lord had saved them from the French and the Spanish.

Finally, he pointed out three steps that God took to deliver the Israelites:

1. He gave them a heart to look to Him for deliverance.

2. He gave them a spirit of courage and resolution to attempt their own deliverance.

3. Then, through the instrumentality of Moses, He delivered them from their oppressors.

SET APART TO BE A HOLY PEOPLE

In summarizing his sermon, Rev. Johnson reminded his hearers that "Israel was called and set apart for God . . . that they might be to him a holy people. . . .

"And let us never forget, that our forefathers left the dear delights of their native country, and fled to the inhospitable deserts of America, — not for worldly wealth and honours, pomp or pleasures; but for the glorious cause of liberty and undefiled religion; — amply to enjoy their civil and religious rights and liberties; — to promote the cause of truth and righteousness; to secure the blessings, and promote the great, everlasting interests of the Kingdom of God.

"It well becomes us to remember how they taught, how they lived, and how affectionately, living and dying, they recommended to us, the glorious cause of liberty, and of pure incorrupt Christianity."

As you consider Rev. Johnson's Fast Day Sermon, which was so influential in his day, do you see analogies to our own time? Should we not also be wary of the gradual encroachments of governmental power over *our* rights? Should we not be wary of every attempt to exercise power beyond right — beyond the bounds laid down in our Constitution? Put your thoughts into an essay on how the lessons in Johnson's Fast Day Sermon apply to our own times.

STEP FIVE:
ORIGINAL THOUGHT

Read pp. 413–429 of your text on the Stamp Act Congress and then pp. 432–438 on the Non-Importation Agreement. Consider the question asked in the margin of p. 420: "What kind of foundation for erecting American unity?" Should the delegates rest the liberties of the colonies only on their charters, or was something more needed to make the foundation of their rights secure?

Note that the views of Christopher Gadsden of South Carolina finally prevailed in this matter. Note also the role Gadsden played in recommending to the South Carolina Assembly that it send a delegation to the Congress at New York, as well as the active part taken by the South Carolina delegation at the Congress. (See p. 416 of your text)

Note the sequence of events at the Congress:

• First, they drew up and agreed to a declaration of their rights. They knew this was the first thing to do. Once laid out on paper and agreed to by the delegates, it would form the basis of the other papers to be drawn up and sent to Great Britain.

• Second, they drew up a petition to the King, setting forth their affectionate regard for him, their pride in being part of the British empire and contributing to its prosperity — and then stating their rights under the Constitution. Note that they claimed the right *voluntarily* to grant to the King the support he requested, and that above all, they claimed "the invaluable rights of taxing ourselves and trial by our peers." They asked his Majesty's protection of these rights which dated from Magna Charta.

• Third, they sent a memorial to the House of Lords, also outlining their constitutional rights.

- Lastly, they petitioned the House of Commons, courteously expressing their "deepest concern and surprise" concerning the "burdensome restrictions" on their trade and, above all, the Stamp Tax.

Note the *tone of appeal* in their wording: they most "ardently implore the attention of the honorable house" to their "united and dutiful" explanation of their circumstances and their "supplications for relief" from regulations that "have already involved this continent in anxiety, confusion and distress." These and other similar passages are an appeal to the House of Commons to consider the hardships the colonists are experiencing as a result of the Stamp Act, to bring it home to the members in a vivid way so as to arouse their sympathies.

The *reasonable* and *respectful* tone of the document vividly portrays the injustice of the new parliamentary measures together with the justice of their constitutional arguments for redress. (Nor did they hesitate to point out that it was in the best interest of Great Britain that the proposed trade regulations and the Stamp Tax be rescinded. (See your text, pp. 428–429)

STEP SIX:

WHAT CHRISTIAN PRINCIPLES AND IDEAS IDENTIFY THE AMERICAN POLITICAL UNION?

1. The clergy led the colonists in opposition to the Stamp Tax and in defense of their rights to "life, liberty and property" as God-given and not man bestowed. The patriotic clergy held that civil government was the minister of God to the people for their good and that when rulers departed from this standard and ruled arbitrarily without regard to the laws of God and to the harm of the people, they should be resisted because "Tyranny is no government." As Rev. Jonathan Mayhew said: "The Gospel promises liberty and permits resistance." (*Union*, p. 412)

2. One of the most influential sermons of the time was Rev. Stephen Johnson's Fast Day Sermon of December 18, 1765, in which he contrasted the unjust slavery of the Israelistes in Egypt with the enslaving measures of the British ministry over its American colonies. He maintained that no obedience is due to arbitrary, unconstitutional edicts because they violated the English Constitution that King and Parliament were sworn to uphold. He also maintained that no obedience was due to such laws by the law of God. "A slavish non-resistance and passive obedience, cannot comport with the will of God" because this would only support "misrule and tyranny." (See p. 65 of this *Study Guide*)

3. Lay leaders of the opposition, like James Otis and Samuel Adams in Massachusetts and Patrick Henry in Virginia, mobilized resistance to the Stamp Act and urged union of the colonies on this issue. Henry's *Virginia Resolves* were an important declaration of constitutional principles that were shared by the other colonies. (See *Union*, pp. 402–404)

4. At the Stamp Act Congress the colonies became "a bundle of sticks, which could neither be bent nor broken." They united to draw up a declaration of rights and grievances and humbly petitioned the King and Parliament for a redress of their grievances. (See pp. 422–429)

5. The colonies also voluntarily entered into non-importation agreements (p. 436). "The fair daughters of America [also] imbibed the same spirit with her sons, and were not less exemplary in various instances of self-denial" in what they viewed as the sacred cause of liberty. (p. 437)

6. After thorough debate in Parliament and an appearance by Benjamin Franklin to answer questions, the Stamp Act was repealed on March 18, 1766 under the new prime minister William Pitt. (p. 438) "The colonists had in almost every way resisted the stamp-act, entirely prevented its operation, and transacted their maritime and civil affairs without stamps, directly in the face of the law, indeed as though the law had not required the use of them, or had never existed." (p. 438)

7. They did so because they were convinced that their rights under God's Law of Nature and the English Constitution had been violated. That the law was unconstitutional was reiterated in *all* the colonial declarations, resolves, memorials, remonstrances and petitions sent to King, Lords and Commons.

RESISTANCE TO THE TOWNSHEND ACTS

*They have also healed the hurt of my people slightly, saying
Peace, peace; when there is no peace.*
(Jeremiah 6:14)

After the Stamp Act was revoked, American patriots began to see that a union of all the colonies was "the means of perpetuating their own liberties." At the same time, British politician Charles Townshend was advocating colonial union of a different kind. His objective was to unite the colonies by: 1) abolishing all their charters; 2) severely circumscribing the powers of their local assemblies; 3) forbidding any general congress of the colonies; 4) and making their governors, judges and attorneys *independent of the colonists* and *dependent on Great Britain* by having the Crown pay their salaries.

"'I would govern the Americans,' said he, 'as subjects of Great Britain; I would restrain their trade and their manufactures as subordinate to the mother country. These our children, must not make themselves our allies in time of war and our rivals in peace." (See *Union,* p. 441)

As the newly-appointed Chancellor of the Exchequer, Townshend pushed through both Houses of Parliament a revenue bill to which the King readily assented. The Townshend Acts "levied a duty on glass, paper, painters' colors, and tea; established a board of customs at Boston for collecting the whole American revenue" which was to be at the disposal of the King to support officers of the Crown in the colonies and "to secure their independence of the local legislatures." (*Ibid.*)

The patriotic leaders made good use of the time between the passage of these acts in the summer of 1767 and the date they were due to go into effect (in November) to *study* the bill, to *write* on the subject so that the public would be well informed, and to *organize* the opposition. (See *Union,* p. 441)

THE MASSACHUSETTS CIRCULAR LETTER

One of the most influential papers drawn up was the Massachusetts *Circular Letter* to the other colonial legislatures. Drafted by Samuel Adams, the document declared that the colonists had both a natural and constitutional right to the free disposal of their property which neither king nor parliament could legally suspend. (See Step Two)

THE FARMER'S LETTERS

Another important paper which was circulated throughout the colonies at this time was John Dickinson's famous *Letters of a Farmer in Pennsylvania to the Inhabitants of the British Colonies.* Dickinson's *Farmer's Letters* helped to educate the people in the fundamental principles at stake in the dispute with Great Britain and warned them of the insidious nature of the Townshend Acts.

"Some people may think this act of no consequence," Dickinson wrote, "because the duties are so small. *A fatal error....* For I am convinced, that the authors of this law would never have obtained an act to raise so trifling a sum as it must do, had they not intended by it to establish a precedent for future use. To console ourselves with the smallness of the duties, is to walk deliberately into the snare that is set for us.... In short, if they have a right to levy a tax of one penny upon us, they have a right to levy a million upon us: for where does their right stop?... 'There is nothing which we can call our own,' or, to use the words of Mr. Locke — 'what property have we in that, which another may, by right, take, when he pleases, to himself?'" (See Step Five)

The educational effort of such patriots as Adams and Dickinson, resulted in the colonies uniting in a non-importation agreement that brought about the repeal of the Townshend Acts — except for the trifling tea tax which Parliament retained *as a symbol of their right to tax the colonies.* Also, still in effect was the Declaratory Act passed earlier after repeal of the Stamp Act. It asserted Parliament's right "to bind the colonies and people of America... in all cases whatsoever." So the great constitutional debate was far from over.

The colonists' efforts to maintain their liberty and local self-government gained the admiration of some Englishmen who were inspired by the Americans' "noble struggle for liberty" and discerned its Christian base. One Englishman wrote prophetically: "The whole Christian world owe you much thanks. The star rising out of your wilderness will become a great luminary and enlighten the whole earth." (*Christian History*, p. 314)

STEP ONE:
PRINCIPLES TO PONDER

1. INDIVIDUAL FREEDOM IS SECURED BY THE RIGHT TO PRIVATE PROPERTY

"Our vigilance and our union, are success and safety. Our negligence and our division, are distress and death.... Let us consider ourselves as men — freemen — Christian freemen — separated from the rest of the world, and firmly bound together by the same rights, interests and dangers.... Let these truths be indelibly impressed on our minds — that we cannot be happy, without being free — that we cannot be free, without being secure in our property — that we cannot be secure in our property, if without our consent, others may, as by right, take it

away...." (John Dickinson, "Farmer's Letter," *Union*, pp. 444–445)

2. PROPERTY IS BOTH A NATURAL AND A CONSTITUTIONAL RIGHT

"It is the glory of the British Constitution, that it hath its foundation in the law of God and nature. It is an essential natural right, that a man shall quietly enjoy, and have the sole disposal of his own property. This right is adopted into the constitution." (Samuel Adams, *Union*, p. 453)

"... the House have humbly represented to the [British] ministry their own sentiments... that it is an essential, unalterable right in nature, engrafted into the British constitution as a fundamental law, and ever held sacred and irrevocable by the subjects within the realm, that what a man has honestly acquired is his own, which he may freely give, but cannot be taken from him without his consent...." (Samuel Adams, The Circular Letter of the Massachusetts Assembly, *Union*, p. 463)

3. DELEGATED POLITICAL POWER MUST BE CONSTANTLY SUPERVISED BY THE PEOPLE

"Every free state should incessantly watch, and instantly take alarm on any addition being made to the power exercised over them." (John Dickinson, *Union*, p. 468)

"Keep an Eagle Eye upon every innovation and stretch of power." (Samuel Adams, *Union*, p. 477)

STEP TWO:
READING FOR LEADING IDEAS

Read *Union*, pp. 440–442 and pp. 448–476.
Note that as the colonists analyzed the new Townshend Acts, they became convinced it was just the Stamp Act all over again — though in a different guise. Therefore, they soon began to mount their opposition. Read the stirring words of some of the patriots who discerned that, as they declared, "the Rubicon is passed." (*Union*, p. 441)

A GREAT CHANGE IN THE POLTICAL POSITION OF THE COLONISTS

Note that a great change in the political position of the colonies took place in 1768: "Hitherto the colonists, in defence of their property, had denied the supremacy of Parliament as based on usurpation; but now, in defence of their privileges, they denied the prerogative of the king. . . ." (p. 448) This change grew out of the Massachusetts Circular Letter, written by Samuel Adams and addressed to the other colonial legislative assemblies. (See your text, pp. 446–449 and p. 463)

PARLIAMENT'S POSITION CLEARLY REVEALED

Parliament reacted rashly to this letter and committed "the gravest mistake . . . made by the [English] government during the entire Revolutionary period." This was to demand that the Massachusetts Assembly rescind its letter. (See p. 449) But this demand, followed by an order that the other colonial assemblies ignore the Letter, was surely providential: It clearly revealed Great Britain's antagonism to the right of local self-government and compelled the colonists to *define* and *declare* their own political position.

THE THREAT OF ARREST AND TRANSPORTATION TO ENGLAND FAILS TO DETER THE PATRIOT LEADERS

The refusal of Massachusetts to rescind the Circular Letter produced a threat from both houses of Parliament stated in a series of resolves, one of which was that the ring-leaders of "the riotous proceedings" in Boston be arrested and transported to England for trial. (See *Union*, p. 450 and the extracts from these Resolves on p. 344)

But, again, these harsh actions providentially drew the colonies closer together and helped them clarify still further the nature of their rights. The *Resolves of the Virginia House of Burgesses,* passed in May 1769, asserted the rights of any colonist in his Majesty's domains to be tried by a jury of his peers in his own locality. (*Union*, p. 466)

EFFECTIVENESS OF RENEWED NON-IMPORTATION AGREEMENTS

Despite threats of reprisals from the British ministry, the colonists did not hesitate to enter once again into non-importation agreements which proved so effective that British merchants, faced with financial disaster, petitioned Parliament for repeal of the Townshend Acts.

REPEAL OF THE TOWNSHEND ACTS

The Acts were repealed with the exception of the one establishing a tax on imported teas. Samuel Adams realized it would be dangerous to allow the remaining tax on tea to go unchallenged. Not to oppose it was to give tacit consent that Parliament did indeed possess the legal authority to tax the colonists.

Because the tea tax was so small, however, many people were disposed to let the matter drop. Samuel Adams feared that to do so was to be lulled into a false security, an elusive sense of peace where there was none (Jeremiah 6:14). So he worked to keep the issue alive in newspaper articles and correspondence with other patriotic leaders throughout the colonies. (See your text, pp. 469–474)

STEP THREE: QUESTIONS FOR INVENTION

1. In addition to entering into non-importation agreements as a protest against the Townshend Acts, what other important steps did Boston suggest that the colonists take? (See *Union*, pp. 441–442)

2. In the Massachusetts Circular Letter, on what grounds did Samuel Adams deny the King's prerogative? (See *Union*, pp. 449)

3. In his Letter to the London Agent of Massachusetts, Samuel Adams said that the British Constitution had its foundation in what two fundamental laws? What was the source of each? (*Union*, p. 453)

4. What was the result of Parliment's act for suspending the New York Assembly until it should comply with the Acts of Parliament? Could the Assembly be said to exist any more, except by Parliamentary permission? If suspension of other colonial assemblies were to follow, what would happen to the authority of these assemblies? (See your text, p. 460 and also p. 344, for a pertinent extract from the Act)

5. What was an "American Episcopate"? Why were the colonists of Massachusetts Bay so worried that England would impose it on their colony? (See your text, pp. 461–462 and review John Adams' Letter to Dr. Jedediah Morse, on pp. 41-44)

6. *Non-importation agreements* proved an effective tool for opposing both the Stamp Act and the Townshend Acts. An internal version of these non-importation agreements as a tool of protest would be the *boycott.* Can you think of ways in which boycotting has been useful today?

7. What would be a better method than the boycott for stopping the spread of offensive reading

material and television programs? Does the real source of the problem lie in the *demand* for this kind of material? Is there a character problem that needs to be addressed?

8. The non-importation agreements of our forefathers were agreements of private citizens — merchants and traders, even as boycotts are usually undertaken by private groups today. But what about the embargo — a *governmental* act that forbids the landing of certain foreign merchandise into this country or forbids that certain domestic merchandise be sent to a foreign country? Is there ever a time when such embargoes are useful?

9. Following the line of reasoning of John Locke, Samuel Adams maintained in the Boston Gazette, in 1771, that every man was born naturally free; that nothing could make a man a subject of any commonwealth, but his actually entering into it by express promise and compact.

When the colonists entered into a compact with the kings of England (through their Charters) did they, Samuel Adams asked, enter into an express promise to be subject to the absolute control of "the parent state"? (See *Union*, pp. 471–472)

STEP FOUR:

FURTHER STUDY OF PRINCIPLES
AND LEADING IDEAS

For a deeper understanding of how union developed in America between 1766–1770, read *Christian History*, Vol. I, pp. 302–315 and *Union*, p. 343 on the Declaratory Act. Note that it declared "that the said colonies and plantations in America have been, and of right ought to be, subordinate unto, and dependent upon the imperial Crown and Parliament of Great Britain; and that the King's Majesty, by and with the advice and consent of the Lords Spiritual and Temporal, and Commons . . . had, hath, and of right ought to have, full power and authority to make laws and statutes of sufficient force and validity to bind the colonies and people of America, subjects of the Crown of Great Britain, in all cases whatsoever." It also declared "null and void" any laws or statutes passed in the colonies which denied "the power and authority of the Parliament of Great Britain" over the colonies.

Despite its stern wording, many colonists paid little attention to the act. No colonial laws had in fact been repealed and all the taxes imposed by the Townshend Act has been revoked — except, of course, the one on tea — so it seemed to most people

that everything was back to normal. But not to the patriot leaders, like Samuel Adams. He knew that even William Pitt, a statesman sympathetic to America, had "asserted for Parliament the right of governing, as emphatically as he denied the right to tax." (*Christian History,* Vol. I, p. 302)

Adams saw that because of the Declaratory Act, which was still in effect, further conflict with the Mother Country would be bound to resume — as it had over the Townshend Acts and the attempt of Parliament to suspend the New York assembly until it complied with their act requiring it to provide quarters for British troops. (See *Union,* p. 344 for the Act Suspending New York Assembly — 1767, and the Quartering Act of 1765, pp. 342–343)

BUILDING AN INTELLIGENT PUBLIC OPINION

Although the patriot leaders wanted to rouse the spirit of resistance to tyranny in the people, they also realized how important it was to restrain unthinking and unlawful mob action by a people deeply resentful of British tyranny. James Otis gave "a spirited denunciation of mobs" at a Boston town meeting declaring that "were the burdens of the people ever so heavy, or their grievances ever so great, no possible circumstances, though ever so oppressive, could be supposed sufficient to justify private tumults and disorders, either to their consciences before God, or legally before men; that their forefathers, in the beginning of the reign of Charles I, for fifteen years together, were continually offering up prayers to their God, and petitions to their king for redress of grievances, before they would betake themselves to any forcible measures. . . ." (See *Christian History,* Vol. I, p. 304)

A NEW METHOD OF POLITICAL AGITATION

Clearly, American Whigs, as the defenders of Constitutional liberty, worked to build their cause "on the foundation of an intelligent public opinion" and, as historian Richard Frothingham discerned, "This was a new and an American method of political agitation." (*Ibid.,* p. 325)

Frothingham also remarks that the appeals of the popular leaders had "an elevation of sentiment so common and so continuous as to constitute a feature of the revolutionary struggle. Thus, 'The Farmer's Letters', [of John Dickinson], addressed to 'The American People,' imbued with a sentiment of union — say, 'You are assigned by Divine Providence, in the appointed order of things, the protectors of unborn ages, whose fate depends on your virtue.'" (See *Christian History,* p. 305 and *Union,* p. 447)

COMPLETING THE CHAIN OF UNION

As the colonists became convinced that "American liberty must be entirely of American fabric," they joined together in support of the Massachusetts Circular Letter and the non-importation movement. When North Carolina entered the non-importation agreement, it was said: "This completes the chain of union throughout the continent for the measure of non-importation and economy." (*Christian History,* Vol. I, p. 313)

STEP FIVE:
ORIGINAL THOUGHT

John Dickinson first came to the forefront of patriotic thinkers and writers with his *Letters of a Farmer in Pennsylvania to the Inhabitants of the British Colonies.* He participated prominently in every major political development that took place thereafter in America from the Stamp Act Congress of 1765 to the Constitutional Convention of 1787.

THE PENMAN OF THE REVOLUTION

Dickinson became known as "the Penman of the Revolution." It was he who drafted the *Resolutions* of the Stamp Act Congress and, as a delegate to the Continental Congress, the *Declaration of Resolves* (1774) and *A Declaration of the Causes of Taking Up Arms* (1775).

Although Dickinson resisted the idea of independence in 1776 (he believed the colonies should not abandon an old "house" before building a new one), he marched to the defense of his country. Later, when Congress desired to draw up the *Articles of Confederation* to unite the newly-independent states, it was Dickinson who was given the task of helping to draft this new document of union.

After military service during the war, Dickinson served as President of Pennsylvania (1782–1785). He then retired to his Delaware estate, but was soon called back to public life to attend the Annapolis Convention of 1786. The next year he was sent as a delegate from Delaware to the Constitutional Convention. Here he was an able supporter of a stronger national union. After the convention, John Dickinson wrote *The Letters of Fabius,* a series of essays explaining and defending the proposed Constitution.

DICKINSON'S RELIGIOUS BACKGROUND

Dickinson was a lawyer by profession and had studied law at the Middle Temple in London. He was raised a Quaker, but became an Episcopalian later in life. For more on his life, see M. E. Bradford, *A Worthy Company — Brief Lives of the Framers of the United States Constitution* (published by Plymouth Rock Foundation, P. O. Box 425, Marlborough, New Hampshire 03455) and Catherine Drinker Bowen, *Miracle at Philadelphia: The Story of the Constitutional Convention, May to September 1787,* available from your local bookstore or from the Foundation for American Christian Education, Box 27035, San Francisco, California 94127.

His Christian convictions are evident in the *Farmer's Letter* that appears in your text (pp. 443–447), particularly in his vision of Americans united as "Christian freemen" and of their role, under Divine Providence, as "the protectors of unborn ages." These words of Dickinson's are yet another example of the Founding Fathers' concern for their posterity.

JOHN DICKINSON'S KEEN POLITICAL INSIGHT

Also evident in this *Letter* is his keen political insight. Note his discernment of the significance of the duties imposed by the Townshend Acts. He tells why it would be "a fatal error" to believe that just because the taxes were small, the Act was of no consequence. Dickinson saw that to be lulled into complacency would be fatal, that "Slavery is ever preceded by sleep."

Write a short essay on Dickinson's paper relating it to his character as a Christian and discussing the character of the American union he proposed.

STEP SIX:
WHAT CHRISTIAN PRINCIPLES AND IDEAS IDENTIFY THE AMERICAN POLITICAL UNION?

1. The colonists increasingly saw themselves as a band of Christian brethren, "Christian freemen — separated from the rest of the world, and firmly bound together by the same rights, interests and dangers." (*Union,* p. 444)

2. They also saw themselves as having the Providential duty to defend not only their rights, but those of their posterity. (*Union,* p. 447)

3. Their non-importation agreements, entered into voluntarily, were an effective means of resistance to the Townshend Acts. (See *Union,* p. 467)

4. The colonists increasingly defended their rights not merely under their Charters or the British Constitution, but under the Higher Law that lay behind all human laws — the Law of God. (See *Union*, p. 453)

5. The New England colonists were not only united in their opposition to the Townshend Act, but to an American Episcopate which would rob them of their religious rights. (See *Union*, pp. 461–462)

6. Leaders like Samuel Adams and John Dickinson saw that there could be no peace with England until she abandoned the notion of Parliamentary authority over the colonies "in all cases whatsoever." They knew that the Declaratory Act had been issued to make clear this notion of Parliamentary supremacy over colonial governments and that this was the reason for retaining the tea tax after all the other taxes under the Townshend Acts had been repealed. (*Union*, pp. 343 and 453)

LESSON ELEVEN

AMERICAN
POLITICAL ACTION

Where the spirit of the Lord is, there is liberty.
(II Corinthians 3:17)

This lesson explores the origin and development of the Committees of Correspondence which became one of the most effective methods for achieving American political union throughout the continent.

The idea was first put into practice by Samuel Adams in 1772, to protest Great Britain's decision to make colonial judges and other officers dependent on the Crown for their salaries. But it had been suggested six years earlier by the Rev. Thomas Mayhew in a letter to James Otis (June 1766). "You have heard of the communion of churches," Mayhew wrote early one Sunday morning explaining that "while I was thinking of this in my bed, the great use and importance of a communion of colonies appeared to me in a strong light. Would it not be decorous for our Assembly to send circulars to all the rest, expressing a desire to cement union among ourselves? A good foundation for this has been laid by the [Stamp Act] Congress at New York; never losing sight of it may be the means of perpetuating our liberties...." (*Union*, p. 440)

The Boston patriots made some use of this suggestion in their circular letters, but it was Samuel Adams who created an ongoing system of Committees of Correspondence in 1772, at first only in Massachusetts, with correspondence between its towns.

In Step Two, you will be studying the stirring three-part report prepared by the first Committee of Correspondence in Boston, on *The Rights of the Colonists as Men, as Christians, and as Subjects.* Written by Samuel Adams, Dr. Joseph Warren, and Benjamin Church, it was "the boldest and most comprehensive summary of the American cause." Sent to all the towns in Massachusetts, it soon gained widespread support, with many approving letters sent off to Boston from the towns which formed their own committees of Correspondence as the report suggested.

Soon the idea extended to correspondence between colonial legislatures. When this proved not sufficiently effective, correspondence was begun again at the local level with correspondence between counties in each colony. Then "The county committees, in turn, chose certain members from their committees to correspond with the other colonies and call a provincial congress when desirable." (See chart showing the development of the Committees of Correspondence, on p. 80 of this *Study Guide*. The development of these committees is taken up in detail in Step Five.)

The committees of correspondence grew "into a mighty tree" and proved an excellent way to by-pass tyrannical government and its proceedings, uniting the people throughout the colonies in *constitutional resistance* to unconstitutional measures. These committees were, says historian John Fiske, "nothing less than the beginning of the American union." (*Union*, p. 478)

"In his own colony," says Edward D. Collins, "Adams was untiring and invaluable in setting the system in operation. His friends doubted the expediency of his plan and the measure had lukewarm support, but the men who feared or doubted were overborne and those who apprehended failure were silenced by the success with which Adams kept things moving. The Boston committee of correspondence has been likened to a political party manager. It provided for regular meetings, consulted with other similar bodies in the vicinity, stimulated the spread of committees in surrounding towns, kept up a correspondence with them, prepared political matter for the press, circulated it in newspapers and broadsides, matured political measures, created and guided public sentiment...." (*Union*, p. 492)

These Committees of Correspondence were particularly effective in their opposition to the Tea Act and preventing the landing of the tea at Boston. (See Step Five)

STEP ONE:
PRINCIPLES TO PONDER

1. THE BOSTON PATRIOTS RESPECTED THE PRINCIPLE OF LOCAL SELF-GOVERNMENT

"Anxious, however, as the originators of the measure were for its success, they did not follow the report [on the Rights of the Colonists] into the country, and speak there in public meetings in its favor. I have not seen the mention of a single address, delivered by a Boston orator to a political gathering in the other towns, during the ten years' controversy before the war.... The Boston leaders relied on correspondence and the press in the promotion of their objects." (Richard Frothingham, *Union*, p. 487)

2. THE PRINCIPLE OF THE COMMITTEES OF CORRESPONDENCE WAS "COOPERATION AT TERMINAL POINTS"

"It is obviously a principle and not a prototype that we have to deal with. The principle is very simple, and very fundamental. It was correspondence, with cooperation at terminal points.... It was not merely a channel through which public opinion might flow; it created public opinion and played upon it to fashion events.... It initiated measures, and its activities comprehended legislative, executive and judicial functions. It was the germ of a government." (Edward D. Collins, *Union*, p. 490)

3. RIGHTEOUS RESISTANCE TO TYRANNY IS SEEN AS THE COLONISTS' CHRISTIAN DUTY

"RESOLVED, That it is the opinion of this town, that a despotic arbitrary government is the kingdom of this world, as set forth in the New Testament, and is diametrically opposite to the establishment of Christianity, in a society, and has a direct tendency to sink a People into a state of ignorance and irreligion; and that if we have an eye to our own and posterity's happiness (not only in this world but the world to come) it is our duty to oppose such a government... and it is at this time eminently incumbent upon one and all, to seek at the throne of the great GOD, for those special and remarkable interpositions of divine providence, grace and mercy, which have so often saved New England from both public and private distress and misery...." (Proceedings of the town of Petersham, *Union*, pp. 495–496)

STEP TWO:
READING FOR LEADING IDEAS

It was at a town meeting held in Faneuil Hall, Boston on November 2, 1772 that Samuel Adams proposed, as historian Frothingham explains, a means "to consolidate the popular party by an organization to be known as committees of correspondence, to constitute an authentic medium for an interchange of views, and for promoting concert of action. Samuel Adams had long mused on the feasibility of this scheme...." (*Union*, p. 479) He was convinced that if the towns of Massachusetts would take the first step, such committees would soon extend from colony to colony "and, thus united, the people would be enabled to resist successfully the measures of the ministry." (*Ibid.*)

He moved "that a committee of correspondence be appointed, to consist of twenty-one persons, to state 'the rights of the colonists, and of this province in particular, as men, as Christians, and as subjects; to communicate and publish the same to the several towns in this province and to the world, as the sense of this town, with the infringements and violations thereof that have been, or from time to time may be made; also requesting of each town a free communication of their sentiments on this subject.'" (p. 481)

THE BOSTON COMMITTEE'S THREE-PART REPORT

The motion was unanimously carried and a committee immediately formed which began to draft a three-part report, stating the rights of the colonists, the infringements of those rights by Great Britain, and a letter of correspondence to the other towns inviting their response.

It naturally fell to Adams to outline the fundamental political principles and rights of the colonies in Part One. In it, he reiterated the argument of no taxation without representation denying "that there could be any representation in parliament that would render taxation of the colonies by that body legal" and characterizing Magna Charta as a declaration of inherent, natural rights of *all* British subjects including the British colonists.

Part Two, assigned to Adams' good friend and helper, Dr. Joseph Warren, detailed the violations of colonial rights under ten headings. Warren condemned Parliament for assuming the power to bind the colonies "in all cases whatsoever" and to try Americans in English courts of admiralty set up in America thus depriving the colonists "of their inestimable right to trials by juries; which has ever been justly considered as the grand bulwark and security of English property." Prohibiting the colonies from erecting iron foundries for manufacturing their own iron was also condemned as a violation of the colonists' God-given right "to make use of our skill and industry in producing the necessaries and conveniences of life." (See *Union*, pp. 482–484)

Part Three of the report, consisting of an explanatory letter from the Boston Committee to the other towns, was written by Benjamin Church. It briefly summarized Parts One and Two and then "invited a free communication. . . to Boston" of the sentiments of the towns with regard to the report. (See *Union*, p. 484)

An important point to note is that while this report was "the boldest and most comprehensive summary of the American cause," it was "remarkably free from passion; and, stating principles and their violation with simplicity, it calmly addressed reason. . . ." (*Ibid.*) Adams and his associates were interested in generating constructive action not destructive acts of thoughtless indignation.

CHRISTIAN CHARACTER OF THE TOWNS' RESPONSES

Note the Christian character of the responses of the different towns to the Boston Committee's Report. (See your text, p. 488 and pp. 493–496) It is also noteworthy that it took only a month for 45 towns to respond with hearty endorsements of the report. Within a week thereafter, 80 towns had responded! As the replies poured into Boston, it was decided to collect them all and publish them in a volume so that "posterity may know what their ancestors did in the cause of freedom." (p. 488)

TEACHING THE PRINCIPLES OF LIBERTY TO EACH GENERATION

These patriots knew how important it was to teach each generation the *principles* and *acts* of their forefathers in the cause of freedom so that they, too, would be moved to defend their heritage of liberty and self-government whenever it might be threatened. They knew that the rising generation would need to learn how to follow in their footsteps and "keep an Eagle Eye upon every innovation and stretch of power, in those that have the rule over us." (Part III of the Boston Report, *Union*, p. 486) Our forefathers knew that, as Samuel Adams wrote, "it can never be expected that a people, however numerous will form and execute a wise plan to perpetuate their liberty, when they have lost the Spirit and feeling of it." (*Union*, p. 520)

". . . THIS LAND, WHERE THE GOSPEL HATH FLOURISHED"

We can also see in their writings the steadfast faith of our forefathers that "GOD will not suffer this land, where the gospel hath flourished, to become a slave of the world," but that He would, in his merciful Providence, raise up "witnesses of the truth, and in his own time spirit his people to stand for his cause and deliver them." (*Union*, p. 496)

Now read *Union*, pp. 478–496; and, if you have it, *Christian History*, Vol. I, pp. 365–370 on Samuel Adams' paper "The Rights of the Colonists as Men, as Christians and as Subjects."

STEP THREE:

QUESTIONS FOR INVENTION

1. The Committees of Correspondence begun by Samuel Adams grew "into a mighty tree" uniting the colonies in *constitutional resistance* to unconstitutional measures. Do you think forming such committees today would help to unite American Christians in their opposition to unconstitutional laws? If so, how could this be done?

2. Could national congresses and conventions of these committees be called to discuss current issues that violate our constitutional principles? What kind of documents could such congresses produce?

3. What are seven fundamental principles that Samuel Adams stated in his Rights of the Colonists? (See *Union*, p. 482)

4. What three major violations of the American colonists' natural and constitutional rights are stated in Part Two of the Boston Report? (See *Union*, pp. 483–484)

5. What can political action groups learn today from the *tone* of the Boston Report that would help them in drawing up position papers, letters to congressmen, etc.? (See *Union*, p. 484)

6. Is it the duty of a government to provide work for the people who live under it? If not, what is its duty? (*Union*, p. 484)

7. In the *Farmer's Letter*, you will recall that John Dickinson warned that "Slavery is ever preceded by sleep." Similarly, Boston's Letter of Correspondence (Part III of the Boston Report of 1772) also makes the point that it is dangerous to "doze" or to sit "supinely indifferent on the brink of destruction." What qualities of thought and character did the *Farmer's Letter* and the Boston *Letter* hold up as necessary to the perpetuation of liberty? (See your text, pp. 444, 447, 486)

8. The Boston leaders, like Samuel Adams and James Otis, showed great faith in local self-government and made no move to interfere with it by attempting to thrust themselves into the political process in any other town. "The report was to be its own orator" and was designed solely to educate in principles and impart information on the current state of affairs, urging others of like mind to join with Boston.

What about the validity of some Political Action Committees today which, though outsiders to a particular state or community, finance and promote local candidates? Is this kind of political action a good thing? If not, why not?

9. Historian Richard Frothingham writes of the communities "planted under Christian influences, fixed in habits of personal independence . . . whose young men were trained in civil affairs in the town-meeting." (*Union*, p. 487) How useful today is the town meeting concept as a forum for political discussion? Could town meetings of citizens concerned about local political problems help to educate citizens on the proper constitutional solutions to these problems?

10. Would town meetings held in high schools with students investigating issues and speaking pro and con on these issues be a good idea? What would be necessary for this to work properly?

STEP FOUR:

FURTHER STUDY OF PRINCIPLES AND LEADING IDEAS

Read pp. 496–503 and p. 521 in your text. Consider the fact that despite doubts by some of the patriots that the idea of Committees of Correspondence would work and despite the general public apathy on the subject, Samuel Adams courageously persisted in defending the idea as the perfect means to effect union within Massachusetts and then on an inter-colonial basis.

Adams remained a tower of strength even though confronted by doubt and discouragement around him. (See Frothingham's stirring account of the development of unity among the colonies through the Committees of Correspondence and Adams' role as their catalyst in *Christian History*, Vol. I, pp. 322–325)

THE COLONISTS RESIST THE TEA TAX

By 1773, ships loaded with tea were sent from England to four ports: Boston, Charleston, New York and Philadelphia. But Adams had done his work well. Through the Committees of Correspondence that were established in the other colonies, there was now an educated public opinion on the constitutional principle at stake. "The determination of the Americans not to pay a tax levied by a body in which they were not represented was as fixed as the purpose of the king to collect the duty on tea. . . ." (*Christian History*, Vol. I, p. 328)

In early October, a group of Philadelphia patriots circulated an "Address to the Tea Commissioners" pleading with them to decline to accept the tea.

ALL EYES WERE FIXED UPON BOSTON

The Boston patriots then held several meetings at Faneuil Hall, "adopted the Philadelphia resolves, and requested the consignees to resign; but met with a peremptory refusal. Similar meetings were held in New York and Charleston. In the latter city, the consignees of the tea resigned and were warmly thanked for their patriotic act." But in Boston, the consignees in refusing to resign, fixed all eyes upon the town. Under the leadership of Samuel Adams, the committee of correspondence met to draft a Circular Letter to the other committees "reviewing in calm tone, but in strong terms, the question between the colonies and Great Britain." (*Ibid.*, p. 330) The Bostonians continued to press the consignees to resign, but elsewhere there were fears that love of money might prove too strong. A letter from a Philadelphian, printed in Boston, said: "All we fear is that you will shrink at Boston. May God give you virtue enough to save the liberties of your country." (*Ibid.*)

The struggle went on for a month. Finally on November 28 a tea ship arrived in Boston harbor, followed by two more several days later. Adams and his fellow patriots now asked that the tea be sent back in the ships that brought it. But the staunch royalist governor, Gov. Hutchinson, refused to give the ships permission to leave until they had discharged their cargo of tea.

On December 16, a great meeting was held at the Old South Meeting House which was attended by people from Boston and its environs — merchants, yeomen, gentlemen. Francis Rotch, the owner of the tea ship *Dartmouth* was asked to get a pass for his vessel from Governor Hutchinson and return to London with his tea cargo. The meeting adjourned at 3 o'clock, but reconvened at six when Rotch returned to Old South. There were so many people in attendance in the church that many had to stand in the street. Rotch explained that the Governor had again refused to allow his vessel to leave the harbor.

There were, says Frothingham, "slight manifestations of disorder" at these words, but one of the patriots, Thomas Young, reminded them that Rotch "was a good man who had done all that was in his power to gratify the people; and they were enjoined to do no harm to his person or his property." Rotch then told them he could not attempt to leave the port with the tea still on board as this "would prove his ruin." For his own security, he felt he had no choice but to land the tea.

Quietly, Samuel Adams said: "This meeting can do nothing more to save the country." There was a war-whoop at the door, echoed in the galleries. As the people left the church, they went down to the wharf where three ships containing the tea were anchored. For days the patriots had been guarding the vessels lest the tea be clandestinely landed. A party of patriots boarded the three ships, warning the officers and customs official to keep away. Then they "unlaid the hatches, hoisted the chests of tea on deck, cut them open and hove the tea overboard." (*Ibid.*, pp. 332–333)

The extraordinary thing about the action was that it was done in a quiet and orderly fashion. "No other property was injured; no person was harmed; no tea was allowed to be carried away. . . ." Even Governor Hutchinson admitted later that "The whole, was done with very little tumult." (*Ibid.*) In this, the boarding party were doubtless reflecting the views of Samuel Adams and the other patriot leaders — that they do only what had to be done. As John Scollay, a Boston selectman who participated in the "Tea Party" said: "We do console ourselves that we have acted consti-tutionally," *i.e.*, that they "did no more than was necessary, under the circumstances, to defeat the design of landing the teas." (*Ibid.*) (Also, although not mentioned in the text, it is a fact that the colonists later reimbursed the tea companies for their losses.)

As you will learn, in the next lesson, this act brought upon the city a severe penalty — The Boston Port Bill, by which the British blockaded Boston harbor. But this only served, providentially, to unite the colonists still further, and produced calls for a general congress of all the colonies.

How Best to Defend Christian Rights

Throughout these stirring events, in which Samuel Adams played a prominent role, he never lost sight of certain important objectives. Rosalie J. Slater writes: "His concern was to educate his fellow Colonists to reason out their political convictions from the standpoint of their Christian rights. He knew that, in the tradition of freemen, they must discuss, dispute and debate the implications of their position. Thus it was largely through his tireless efforts that he brought into being the Committees of Correspondence and kept them functioning. . . . It was particularly through his own vigorous participation in the Boston Town Meeting that he encouraged public discussion as well as private correspondence as a means of self-education." (*T & L*, p. 254)

Read also her comments under "Patriotic Letters – Committees of Correspondence," *T & L*, pp. 257–258. Notice how Adams' concern was mainly to *educate* the people in the *principles* involved in the issues. He knew that *backing the authorities down on a particular issue did not necessarily mean victory if the principle behind it were not acknowledged*. Thus, it was important to keep fundamental principles before the people at all times, and it was equally important that any actions the people took in defense of their liberties be consistent with these principles. Based on what you have read about him in this lesson, describe in your own words Samuel Adams' method of political education and political action. How did one relate to the other? What roles did the Committees of Correspondence and the Town Meeting play in Adams' strategy for education and action?

Step Five:
Original Thought

Your Reading Assignment for Step Five is found on pp. 505–519 and also pp. 523–528 of your text.

The development of the Committees of Correspondence beyond the borders of Massachusetts has

THE COMMITTEES OF CORRESPONDENCE

The voluntary communicating of Towns, Counties, and Legislative Assemblies, constitutes political action consistent with and springing from local Self-Government with Union — The American idea of Government." (*Christian History, Vol. II: Christian Self-Government with Union*, p. 478)

COMMUNICATING TOWNS

November 2, 1772: The Town of Boston resolves "That a committee of correspondence be appointed . . . to state the rights of the colonists . . . as men, as Christians, and as subjects; to communicate and publish the same to the several towns in this province . . . with the infringements and violations thereof, as from time to time may be made; also requesting of each town a free communication of their sentiments on this subject." (*Union*, p. 491)

January 1773: [Gov.] Hutchinson reported that 80 or more towns in Massachusetts had committees. (*Union*, p. 492)

"The tea importation opportunely gave the committees a subject for correspondence. . . ." (*Union*, p. 492)

"Here was the nucleus for a local federation. . . . It was the germ of a government, but one that would have been purely local." (*Union*, p. 501)

"So long as it was confined to any one colony the ruling spirit in that colony might dominate it; just so soon as it became intercolonial it broke the bonds of local control." (*Union*, p. 492)

COMMUNICATING ASSEMBLIES

March 12, 1773: Virginia's House of Burgesses appoints a Committee: "Be it resolved, That a standing committee of correspondence . . be appointed . . . to . . . maintain a correspondence with our sister colonies; and the result of such their proceedings from time to time to lay before this House." (*Union*, p. 503)

February 8, 1774: By this time twelve committees of correspondence existed, appointed by the legislative assemblies of every colony except Pennsylvania which, about to adjourn, left the decision to be taken by the next assembly. (See *Union*, p. 513)

Structure of Assembly Committees

1. These committees were chosen from members of the legislative assembly.

2. These assembly committees acted only on the advice or direction of those bodies to which they were responsible.

3. They could not act independently of the assemblies and so were hampered when the assemblies were not in session and the members were dispersed to their homes in different parts of the colony. (See *Union*, p. 514)

COMMUNICATING COUNTIES

June 11, 1774: The Freeholders of Essex County, New Jersey met and appointed a committee. Soon other N.J. counties did the same. (*Union*, p. 516)

Structure of County Committees

1. The inhabitants of towns elected committees of correspondence to communicate with other township committees in their county.

2. A county committee was formed of representatives from these township committees. It would then correspond with other county committees in the province and could call a county meeting or convention.

3. The county committees, in turn, chose certain members from their own committees to correspond with the other colonies and call a provincial congress when desirable.

Superiority of the County Committees

They were always in session and, connected with the popular cause through representation in the general congress (first convened September 5, 1774 in Philadelphia), they were equally effective at either end of the "chain of committees", — the township or the congress.

many instructive lessons for us today. You will note from the chart on the facing page that it did not progress as might have been expected — from towns to counties and then to the legislative assemblies — but from towns within Massachusetts to the legislative assemblies of the other colonies.

THE COMMITTEE OF CORRESPONDENCE WAS ESSENTIALLY A LOCAL INSTITUTION

These official committees of the assemblies were, however, of quite limited jurisdiction and practical usefulness. Nonetheless, they played an important *interim role* in establishing communications between the colonies. But, as Edward D. Collins points out, "The committee of correspondence was essentially a local institution," and the county system of committees of correspondence, which eventually developed, *having no formal links with the official colonial assemblies,* proved to be a far more efficient tool for effecting colonial union beginning at the local township level on up, in an unbroken chain of committees.

Consider whether it might be desirable and possible to establish such a committee of concerned citizens in your town and to encourage other people you know in other towns in your county to start similar committees and correspond with each other on constitutional issues of particular concern in your area.

Would not standing committees always in existence at the township and county level have an edge over committees hastily assembled to pursue a single issue as it arises and which then disbands after that particular battle has been fought? Could they not also serve as a great educational base for their communities and counties and eventually the entire state, presenting in town meeting forums Christian alternatives or answers to problems facing their communities? In other words, they would be in business not just to fight against unjust and unchristian laws but *to advance the Christian idea of man and government* in a constructive manner. Would this not provide a positive, new approach to politics at the local, county and state level?

Committees of correspondence at the township and county levels also could share with each other solutions they have found for privately funded and staffed welfare groups. Many such efforts are under way and doing much good but are not always publicized in the press. There would seem to be a need for a practical network of committees over the country spreading the good news of what can be and is being done privately to handle these problems and sharing ways and means developed by the different efforts of private citizen groups.

Write an essay discussing how you think a com-

mittee of correspondence might be useful in your town, your county and your state in relation to current political and economic problems and how such committees could deal with them constitutionally — in relation to your state constitution as well as the United States Constitution. Would it not be a good idea to get a copy of your state constitution and read it to find out how it protects your rights?

STEP SIX:

WHAT CHRISTIAN PRINCIPLES AND IDEAS IDENTIFY THE AMERICAN POLITICAL UNION?

1. The Committees of Correspondence, first conceived by Rev. Jonathan Mayhew and put into effect by Samuel Adams in 1772, "grew into a mighty tree" as they extended beyond the borders of Massachusetts and were established throughout the colonies. "The voluntary communicating of Towns, Counties, and Legislative Assemblies, constitutes political action consistent with and springing from local Self-Government with Union — The American idea of Government." (*Union*, p. 478)

2. The report of the Boston Committee in 1772, at Samuel Adams' suggestion, produced a masterly three-part report on: The Rights of the Colonists as men, as Christians and as Subjects; A List of the Infringements and Violations of Those Rights; and A Letter of Correspondence with the Other Towns requesting a free communication of their sentiments as to the common danger facing them all.

This paper was "the most systematic presentation of the American cause" and "covered the whole ground of natural and constitutional rights. It gave to principles, which had been held as abstractions, a practical significance. It considered the relations of man not only as a citizen, but as a Christian, and claimed for him that equality which is the cardinal principle of Christianity. It claimed for him, under law . . . the right to make the laws under which he lives, to select his field of labor and enjoy its fruits, and thus claimed fair play for the industrial energy which has contributed so much to the growth and glory of the country. Its bold theory, incisive criticism, and solid reasoning were admirably calculated to strengthen and direct public opinion." (*Christian History*, Vol. I, p. 321)

3. The Committees of Correspondence united in their opposition to the Tea Tax by refusing to allow the tea to be landed in their ports (Charleston, New

York, Philadelphia — and Boston). "The destruction of the tea at Boston brought the new organization into requisition for the first time in a way both successful and popular.... An opportunity had been created to communicate something of importance to the sister colonies, along with exhortations to stand by the rebellious member and make her cause their own. A second stimulus was not long wanting. The destruction of the tea brought its own penalty in the port act, and the port act, through ... the committees of correspondence was turned into a powerful force, working through popular sentiment for unity of action against the mother country." (*Union*, p. 521)

LESSON TWELVE

CEMENT
OF AMERICAN
UNION

*Behold, how good and how pleasant it is
for brethren to dwell together in unity!*
(Psalm 133:1)

On June 1, 1774, the Port Bill, ordering the blockade of Boston harbor, went into effect "amid the tolling of bells, fasting and prayer.... Multitudes signed a solemn league and covenant against the use of British goods.... Patriotic donations from every colony were on their way to the suffering towns...." (*Union*, p. 533)

One by one the colonies declared their solidarity with Boston's cause making it their own. At a large meeting in New York on July 6, 1774, it was unanimously resolved that the Boston Port Act was "unconstitutional in its principles and dangerous to the liberties of British America; and that, therefore, we consider our brethren at Boston as now suffering in the common cause of these Colonies...." (*Union*, p. 546)

The Resolutions of this meeting also declared that all the colonies should be urged to pass a joint resolution to stop all trading with Great Britain until the Act had been repealed and that a fund be set up immediately for the relief of the inhabitants of the beleaguered town. It was further resolved "that these Resolutions be printed in the public newspapers of this city and transmitted to the different counties in this Colony and and to the Committees of Correspondence for the neighboring Colonies...." (*Ibid.*, p. 546)

A DAY OF PRAYER TO THE ALMIGHTY DISPOSER OF HUMAN EVENTS

Similar resolutions were passed at a meeting of the Freeholders of York County, Virginia, who also "unanimously resolved.... That the first day of September next, or the time of the general Congress, be set apart as a day of prayer and supplication to the Almighty disposer of human events, to direct the Councils of Americans, and so to dispose of the heart of our Sovereign, that a general harmony may be restored to the British Empire." (*Union*, p. 552)

On August 1, 1774, a convention was held in Virginia, attended by the patriotic leaders of the colony, during which it was resolved "that the united wisdom of North America should be collected in a general Congress of all the Colonies..." and deputies were elected to represent Virginia "in the said Congress, to be held at Philadelphia on the first Monday in September next...." (*Union*, p. 554)

THE FIRST CONTINENTAL CONGRESS — 1774

This Congress produced a Declaration of Rights containing ten resolves enumerating the legal rights of the colonies under the English Constitution and listing 11 acts of Parliament that infringed on those rights and must be repealed before harmony could be restored between the colonies and the Mother

Country. "That paper claimed for Americans the immunities of free subjects within the realm of England.... It presents the colonies as united in vital matters of representation, free discussion, free assemblies, and trial by jury, — in a word, self-government." (*Union,* p. 589)

The Non-Importation Association of the United Colonies

The colonies also entered into a non-importation Association, signing the agreement on October 20, 1774. "The Association has been termed a compact formed for the preservation of American rights, — 'a league of the continent, which first expressed the sovereign will of a free nation in America,' — and the commencement of the American Union. It was an embodiment of the sentiment of Union, and of the will of the people on the subject of their commercial relations, — the first enactment, substantially, of a general law by America. For nearly two years the instrument was termed, 'The Association of the United Colonies'...." (*Union,* p. 590)

Lord Chatham Praises the Masterly State Papers of Congress

The masterly state papers produced by the First Continental Congress of 1774 were widely praised for their "soundness, dignity, strength, and purity of style." They were even praised in Great Britain when Lord Chatham, in a speech to the House of Lords, declared that in all his reading and study of the master states of the world, "for solidity of reasoning, force of sagacity, and wisdom of conclusion, under such a complication of circumstances, no nation or body of men can stand in preference to the general congress at Philadephia." (*Union,* p. 596)

A Christian Prologue

The colonies were as one in support of suffering Boston, sending money, goods and heartfelt expressions of Christian sympathy and encouragement. "The noble record portrays the brotherhood that constituted the real union of the colonies. It admits posterity into the heart of the Revolution. It is a Christian prologue grandly spoken on the entrance of the United States into the family of nations....

"The spirit ... was the same, whether they had grown up under charter, proprietary or royal forms of government, and whether the individual or denominational sympathies were Congregational, Presbyterian, Episcopalian or Quaker: underlying all were Christian brotherhood, sympathy in fundamental political ideas, and enthusiasm for the rights of human nature. These sentiments could not be bound by provincial lines. They expressed the yearning for American unity, — and this for the sake of principles as wide in their application as the common humanity. The simple narration of the progress of events show how a noble spirit spread from heart to heart, and from colony to colony, beyond the power of human calculation." (*Union,* p. 597)

Step One:
Principles to Ponder

1. The New England Civil Commonwealths Were Established on the Basis of Christian Principles

"The New England colonists always claimed the liberties of Englishmen. They brought with them the principles that the people are the fountain of political power and that there can be no just taxation without representation.... They brought with them, also, that republican spirit which animated the English Puritans, and their early ideal was the establishing of civil commonwealths on the basis of Christian principles." (Richard Frothingham, *Union,* p. 531)

2. "Free Principles" Developed in Massachusetts for 150 Years

"In Massachusetts, for nearly a century and a half there had been a steady and healthy development of free principles.... Hence, during the ten years of strong reasoning, and firm resolve, and eloquent appeal — from 1764 to 1774 — the acts judged unconstitutional, and contrary to natural and chartered rights, met in this colony with the most determined opposition. It was carried on by men of the Puritan stock.... There was no compromise, by such men, with duty. Hence, in dealing with the small tax on tea, they died not hesitate to destroy the obnoxious herb." (Richard Frothingham, *Union,* p. 533)

3. Consent of the Governed is Invoked by the Freeholders of Fairfax County, Virginia, as a Fundamental Constitutional Principle

"That the most important and valuable part of the British Constitution ... upon which its very existence depends, is the fundamental principle of the people's being governed by no laws to which they have not given their consent by Representatives freely chosen by themselves...." (*Union,* p. 553)

4. ACTIONS TAKEN BY THE VIRGINIA CONVENTION WERE IN THE NAME OF THE PRINCIPLES OF HUMANITY AND BROTHERLY LOVE

"Resolved, That we think ourselves called upon, by every principle of humanity and brotherly affection, to extend the utmost and speediest relief to our distressed fellow-subjects in the Town of Boston. . . ." (*Union*, p. 553)

5. THE ASSOCIATION OF THE UNITED COLONIES WAS FORMED BY COVENANT

"Their covenant was in these words: "We do for ourselves, and the inhabitants of the several colonies whom we represent, firmly agree and associate under the sacred ties of virtue, honor, and love of our country. . . ." (*Union*, p. 589)

STEP TWO:
READING FOR LEADING IDEAS

Read about the effect on the colonies of the Boston Port Act in *Union*, pp. 531–549. You may also wish to consult the eloquent account in *Christian History*, Vol. I, pp. 334–339.

As you go through your Reading Assignment, notice the use Divine Providence made of the Boston Port Bill *to unify the continent* even though the British intended the blockade of Boston's port *as a device to isolate it from the other colonies.* As Richard Frothingham writes: "It had long been a theory [of the British ministry] that the law of diversity was so deeply rooted . . . that anything like real political unity among the colonies would be impossible. . . ." (See *Christian History*, Vol. I, p. 334) It was supposed that the other colonies would leave Boston to suffer alone and would even "accept with pleasure" any benefits that could be derived from her misfortune. Thus, the British were sure that the policy of singling out Massachusetts for punishment would "prove a means of destroying the bond of union." (*Ibid.*, p. 335)

DIVISION EXPECTED, BUT UNION THE RESULT

Instead, this afflictive Act had just the opposite effect. As your text relates: "[The Boston Port Bill] bore severely upon two towns, Boston and Charlestown, which had been long connected by a common patriotism. Their laborers were thrown out of employment, their poor were deprived of bread, and gloom pervaded their streets. But they were cheered and sustained by the large contributions sent from every quarter for their relief, and by the noble words that accompanied them." (*Union*, p. 533) (The list of donors from Fairfax County was headed by George Washington who gave the generous sum of f50. See *Christian History*, Vol. I, p. 338)

The flow of donations to Boston lasted 10 months, and during this time was accompanied by letters from the committees formed to forward the money. Sent to the patriots of Boston, these letters were "more precious than the gifts themselves." (*Union*, p. 597)

The correspondence was "voluminous" and only a small number of the letters found their way into print in the newspapers. For nearly a century, most of them remained in manuscript form. "They were consequently independent expressions of sentiment, one locality not knowing what another locality had written. . . ." (*Union*, p. 597) Yet each wrote in a similar vein of Christian brotherhood and sympathy with Boston.

The Boston Town Meeting of June 14, 1774, expressed warm thanks for the "humanity, sympathy and affection . . . expressed towards this distressed town at this important season. . . ." The Boston Donation Committee's letter to the colony of New Jersey on August 22, expressed gratitude for the "Christian sympathy and generosity of our friends through the Continent." Note their "trust in the Supreme Ruler of the universe, that he will hear our cries, and in his time free us from our present bondage, and make us rejoice in his salvation." (*Union*, pp. 570–571)

VIRGINIA CALLS FOR
A DAY OF FASTING AND PRAYER

Virginia called for a day of prayer and fasting to be observed on the day the Boston Port Bill went into effect, and large congregations filled the churches throughout the colonies on that day.

"The first of June, the day on which the Port Bill was to take place," Jedediah Morse relates, "was appointed to be kept as a day of humiliation, fasting and prayer throughout the colonies, to see the divine direction and aid, in that critical and gloomy juncture of affairs.

Morse explains that the appointing of Fast Days "in times of distress and impending danger, and of celebrating days of public thanksgiving, after having received special tokens of divine favor, has ever prevailed in New-England since its first settlement, and in some parts of other states. These public supplications and acknowledgements to Heaven, at the commencement of hostilities, and during the whole progress of the war, were more frequent than usual, and were attended with uncommon fervour and solemnity. They were considered by the people, as an humble appeal to Heaven for the justness of their cause, and designed to manifest their dependence on the GOD OF HOSTS for aid and success in maintaining it against their hostile brethren.'' (See *T & L*, pp. 264–265)

VIRGINIA'S FAST DAY — JUNE 1, 1774

Richard Frothingham gives an account of the Fast Day (in *Christian History*, Vol. I, p. 337):

"In Virginia the members of the House of Burgesses assembled at their place of meeting; went in procession, with the Speaker at their head, to the church and listened to a discourse. 'Never,' a lady wrote, 'since my residence in Virginia have I seen so large a congregation as was this day [June 1] assembled to hear divine service.' The preacher selected for his text the words: 'be strong and of good courage, fear not, nor be afraid of them; for the Lord thy God, he it is that doth go with thee. He will not fail thee nor forsake thee.' 'The people,' Jefferson says, 'met generally, with anxiety and alarm in their countenances; and the effect of the day, through the whole colony, was like a shock of electricity, arousing every man and placing him erect and solidly on his centre.' These words describe the effect of the Port Act throughout the thirteen colonies.''

THE ROLE OF NEWSPAPERS AND PAMPHLETS IN CRYSTALLIZING PUBLIC OPINION

In addition to letters and articles supporting Boston in colonial newspapers, many pamphlets were published which aided in crystallizing public opinion. By these means, people all over the colonies learned what principles were at stake in the closing of Boston's harbor to all commerce. (See your text, pp. 543–547) These pamphlets also summarized the colonies' other grievances against the Mother Country. In addition to wide circulation in the colonies, they were sent to the colonial agents in Great Britain in the hope that they would make the colonists' case clear to their English brethren.

STEP THREE:

QUESTIONS FOR INVENTION

1. What were the "dangerous" republican tendencies in the colonies that were noted at this time by "sagacious royalists" here and in England? (See *Union*, p. 532)

2. Why did the New England commonwealths view republican government as so important? (See *Union*, p. 531)

3. With what important attitude was their love of liberty connected? (See p. 532)

4. Why did the blockade of Boston have the opposite effect on the sister colonies of Massachusetts to that intended by Parliament? (See p. 536, par. 3)

5. What do you think is the most compelling reason of those cited by Jedediah Morse for the Fast Day of June 1, 1774, and the other Fast Days of the Revolutionary period? (See *Guide*, pp. 85–86)

6. When their external foreign trade was cut off by the Blockade, what important source of support for the Bostonians was activated? (See p. 533)

7. Why was all this intercolonial correspondence expressing "good will, unity of sentiment, and firmness of purpose to resist oppression" commendable, but inadequate to the problem before the colonists? What more was needed? (See p. 549)

STEP FOUR:

FURTHER STUDY OF PRINCIPLES AND LEADING IDEAS

Read pp. 550–570 of your text. Notice the unanimity of the views expressed: 1) that the rights the colonists claim are from their Creator; 2) that until Great Britain redresses the wrongs done to the colonies, importation from and exportation to Great Britain should cease; 3) that the colonies need to consider the best way to secure their rights and liberties; 4) that they are engaged in a common cause with Boston; 5) that no taxation without representation is a "fundamental principle" of the English Constitution"; and 6) their repreated call for "a general Congress" or "a Congress of deputies" from all the colonies.

Note, too, the repeated references to God and His laws, to their relationship to each other as "Christian freemen" and their reliance on God to help them. See particularly the resolutions of the freeholders of York County, Virginia, and their call for a day of prayer and supplication to God "to direct the Councils of the Americans," and also to work on the heart of the King, that harmony might be restored with the Mother Country.

Copy in your notebook all of the religious references you find in these pages, together with their source and approximate date. Do they not illustrate that there was a great religious, as well as political, consensus of opinion in America at this time?

STEP FIVE:
ORIGINAL THOUGHT

After reading the following summary of events that took place at the First Continental Congress of 1774, read pp. 571–599 of your text.

Fifty-five delegates from 12 colonies attended the First Continental Congress held at Philadelphia in 1774 in Carpenter's Hall. (The non-attending colony was Georgia, but she promised to concur with her "sister colonies" in whatever actions they deemed necessary to take to defend the colonies' right to justice under the British Constitution.)

THE DELEGATES WERE
MEN OF UNCOMMON ABILITY

The delegates to this first Continental Congress "were men of uncommon ability" who had come up from the political ranks in their respective colonies. See the interesting sketch of the delegates in your text on pp. 574–575.

Note the *object* of their meeting and their conclusion that to attain this object they needed to draw up a Declaration of Rights "in which the limits of the powers of the colonies and the mother country might be defined." (*Union*, p. 575)

CONGRESS UNITES IN PRAYER

Note also that diversity of religion did not prevent them from opening their sessions with prayer — although it might have done so except for Samuel Adams' tact and inclusive attitude in his handling of this issue. Their need for prayer was brought home to them on the evening of the same day that Samuel Adams had proposed that prayers be offered the next morning by the Philadelphia clergyman, Rev. Jacob Duche. A rumor that British ships were bombarding Boston plunged the delegates into the greatest anxiety.

The next morning, as they met together in an agitated state, Rev. Duche's reading of the Thirty-Fifth Psalm calmed and strengthened them turning their anxiety into exaltation. Then, as John Adams wrote: "[Rev. Duche] unexpectedly to anybody struck out into an extemporary prayer for America, for the congress, for Massachusetts, and especially for Boston, which was so fervent that it filled the bosom of every man present." (*Union*, p. 576)

THE SUFFOLK RESOLVES

Two days later the delegates learned that the rumored bombardment was false, but other rumors of new British acts of tyranny were not. Then, three days later — on September 17 — something of great importance occurred: Paul Revere rode in from Massachusetts bringing Resolutions that had been passed by the towns of Suffolk County — Boston's home county. The *Suffolk County Resolves* were the boldest statement yet made of the rights of the colonists.

"The resolutions declared that a king who violates the chartered rights of his people forfeits their allegiance; they declared the Regulating Act null and void, and ordered all the officers appointed under it to resign their offices at once; they directed the collectors of taxes to refuse to pay over money to Gage's treasurer; they advised the towns to choose their own militia officers...." (See John Fiske, *The American Revolution,* Vol. 1, p. 108, and the extracts from the *Resolves* in your text, pp. 577–581)

What had occasioned these drastic Resolves? Sir Thomas Gage, the military governor of Massachusetts, had begun to fortify Boston Neck, "so as to close the only approach to the city by land. Next day," says historian John Fiske, "the county assize was to be held at Worcester; but 5,000 armed men, drawn up in regular military array, lined each side of the main street, and the unconstitutionally appointed judges were forbidden to take their seats." (Fiske, Vol. I, p. 108)

THE CHARACTER OF DR. JOSEPH WARREN

On the same day, the Suffolk County meeting was held and Samuel Adams' friend, Dr. Joseph Warren, drew up the *Resolves* which were adopted unanimously. With Adams away at the Congress in Philadelphia, Dr. Warren played an active role in directing the affairs of the Boston patriots. Fiske has this to say about Warren's character and contribution to the patriot cause:

"This gentleman — one of a family which has produced thirteen eminent physicians — was graduated at Harvard College in 1759. He had early attracted the attention of Samuel Adams, had come to be one of his dearest friends, and had been concerned with him in nearly all of his public acts of the past seven years. He was a man of knightly courage and courtesy, and his energy and fertility of mind were equalled only by his rare sweetness and modesty. With Adams and [John] Hancock, he was one of the great Massachusetts triumverate of Revolutionary leaders." (*Ibid.,* p. 107)

The boldness and courage expressed in the Suffolk Resolves stirred the hearts of the delegates to the Congress and they voted their thorough approval of them. John Adams was elated, writing in his Diary: "This was one of the happiest days of my life." "This day convinced me that America will support the Massachusetts or perish with her." (*Union,* p. 582) In his letter to his wife, Abigail Adams, he also expressed his joy in "the esteem, the affection shown for the people of Boston and Massachusetts." See also the significant quote from Samuel Adams' letter to Joseph Warren of September 25, 1774 in your text on p. 583.

THE DECLARATION OF RIGHTS

Note that some of the phrases used in this great document were similar to the English Bill of Rights in 1689. (Extracts from the English Bill of Rights are found in *Christian History,* Vol. I, on pp. 44–47) "It contained ten resolves, in which were enumerated the rights that could not be legally taken from them, or altered or abridged by any power whatever; and it specified eleven acts or parts of acts of parliament which were necessary to be repealed, in order to restore harmony between the colonies and Great Britain." (See particularly the four "Intolerable Acts," under "Acts of Tyranny," in your text, pp. 345–347)

THE DESIGN OF PROVIDENCE

All of the resolves in the Declaration of Rights were unanimously adopted except for two. That such a degree of unanimity could be reached by delegates from colonies of such diversity is little short of amazing. Must it not have been brought about by Divine Providence working upon individual hearts first at the local, then the provincial, and finally the national level to bring them at last to this point of union? Says historian Frothingham:

"The time having come for the people to pass from the control of the mother country, the Governor of the Universe, by secret influence on their minds, disposed them to union, and to give to this union the strength of law." (*Union,* p. 598)

THE INDIVIDUAL'S ROLE IN ACHIEVING CONTINENTAL UNION

Consider the many talented individuals who served as links in the continental chain of union: men like Samuel Adams, Dr. Joseph Warren, John Dickinson, Patrick Henry, George Washington. Each brought to his task the unique qualities of his own God-given individuality. As these men used their abilities in the service of Christian self-government and Biblical Christian unity, American union began to take tangible shape and form.

The achievement of continental union would not have been possible without individuals of talent, conviction and Christian character and commitment, individuals willing to move out into the field of political action armed with their convictions and who had practical experience in government gained from a long apprenticeship.

Write an essay on the qualities of character of Samuel Adams, John Dickinson, and Patrick Henry showing their great diversity of abilities, but how each contributed significantly to the achievement of union in some particular and vital manner. (Check your notes made previously on these three men.)

STEP SIX:

WHAT CHRISTIAN PRINCIPLES AND IDEAS IDENTIFY THE AMERICAN POLITICAL UNION?

1. The Boston Port Act united the American colonies two years before they declared their independence from Great Britain.

2. For Massachusetts there was no turning back after the *Suffolk Resolves.* The patriots organized a provincial government and acted independently of the Assembly which could no longer act on their behalf because of Governor Gage's rule.

3. On the national scene, Congress created a body in the Association of the United Colonies, which was "an embodiment of the sentiment of union and of the will of the people on the subject of their commercial relations, — the first enactment, substantially, of a general law by America." (*Union,* p. 590)

4. "... while the old forms of government remained, the Association virtually constituted a new and independent authority, — a government through congresses and committees." (*Union,* p. 598)

5. The papers produced by the Congress "explaining its measures and vindicating the American cause, have been uniformly praised for their soundness, dignity and strength. They drew from William Pitt, the Earl of Chatham, the tribute delivered in the House of Lords.... 'For myself, I must declare and

avow, that . . . for solidity of reasoning, force of sagacity, and wisdom of conclusion, under such a complication of circumstances, no nation or body of men can stand in preference to the general congress at Philadelphia." (*Union*, p. 596)

6. The correspondence between the colonies and beleaguered Boston "portrays the brotherhood that constituted the real union of the colonies. . . . It is a Christian prologue grandly spoken on the entrance of the United Colonies into the family of nations. . . . underlying all [was] Christian brotherhood. . . ." (*Union*, p. 597)

7. The Hand of God in the development of Christian Self-Government with Union in America may be clearly seen in our history (and was acknowledged by such leaders as George Washington and James Madison). Historian Richard Frothingham writes:

"The time having come for the people to pass from the control of the mother country, the Governor of the Universe, by secret influence on their minds, disposed them to union, and to give to this union the strength of law. . . . Indeed, union had not only passed from sentiment into law, but had become power. The Loyalist could not see this. The chain that appeared to the Whigs bright and golden, appeared to the Tories but a rope of sand. . . ." (*Union*, p. 598)

8. The patriots knew they were building for posterity. One of them wrote: "We are now laying the foundation of an American constitution. Let us therefore hold up every thing we do to the eye of posterity. They will probably measure their liberties and happiness by the most careless of our footsteps. *Let no unhallowed hand touch the precious seed of liberty.*" (*Ibid.*, emphasis added)

AFTERWORD

Now that you have finished this study course, turn back to the *Introduction* of *Union* and the questions posed by Miss Hall in the opening paragraph. You will recall that you answered these questions at the beginning of the course. Now answer them again and compare your answers with those you gave previously. Your answers, this time, should reflect much more depth of understanding and documentation than before. Only the last question may give you pause: "Does time, or rapid communication, or increased population or diversity of races and creeds, affect voluntary cooperation?" But consider:

Time

As to the times being different, are not men and women basically the same in our time as in past times? Do they not still possess great potential for good under Divine Providence, since they are made in the Divine Image? But are they not also as capable as ever of great evil because of their proness to sin since the Fall, a fact which our Founding Fathers took into consideration when they framed the state constitutions and our national Constitution. Have we outgrown the government their wisdom gave us?

Communication

Should not the rapid communication of our era *facilitate,* rather than impede, union?

Increased Population

And what about increased population? Does this change our capacity for union? In 1787, the largeness and diversity of the American states at that time led many to believe that a firmer American union would be impossible, but this belief proved to be false.

Diversity of Races

What about the many different races and ethnic minorities that have been welcomed to our nation? Does this make union under our Constitution impossible? Does not the Apostle Paul say: "For there is neither Jew nor Greek, there is neither slave nor free, there is neither male nor female; for you are all one in Christ Jesus." (Galatians 4:28) So is it not possible for all in America to be one as Americans under the same Constitution since it reflects the Christian view of man and government which accords dignity to *all* individuals and freedom of religious expression to all, whether Christians or not?

Charles Bancroft, in his *Footprints of Time,* believed that "America is the common ground on which all the currents, hastening by lightning and by steam, seek again every quarter of the earth with kindly greeting, to renew the relations broken in the original separation of the races, and to cement, by exchanges mutually profitable, a new and better unity of

91

mankind. As the heart in the human body receives the current of blood from all parts of the system, and, having revitalized it, returns it with fresh elements of strength, so America adopts the children of all lands only to return a manhood ennobled by a sense of its own dignity through the practice of a system of self-government which improves the condition and promotes the interest of each while it produces harm to none." (*Christian History,* Vol. I, p. 8)

Diversity of Creeds

What then of diversity of creeds? Is it not the special character of true Christianity to accord toleration to those of other faiths and to seek to win them for Christ by *persuasion,* rather than by force? John Locke wrote: "If the Gospel and the Apostles may be credited, no Man can be a Christian without Charity, and without that Faith which works, not by Force, but by Love...." (*Union,* p. 46)

With regard to Christians specifically, this nation has united them in mutual tolerance and forebearance of each other's different theological views. Said George Washington: "It affords edifying prospects,

indeed, to see Christians of different denominations dwell together in more charity, and conduct themselves in respect to each other, with a more Christian-like spirit than ever they have done in any former age or in any other nation." (*Union,* p. 530)

———

Perhaps, now that you have finished this study course, you may be interested in starting a study group of your own so that you can pass your conviction and knowledge of fundamental principles on to your friends and neighbors or to your business associates. Ideas for conducting such a group are presented in *Suggestions for Study Group Leaders,* on p. XIII of this *Study Guide.* An Answer Key to the *Questions for Invention* and a sample essay for Step Five of *Lesson One* is also available to assist you from the

American Christian History Institute,
P.O. Box 648,
Palo Cedro, California 96073.

Your questions and any comments you may have on this course are welcome.